BUSINESS GUIDEBOOKS

MAIL ORDER

A SMALL BUSINESS GUIDE

Alan & Deborah Fowler

GW00708174

Sphere Reference

MAIL ORDER

A SMALL
BUSINESS GUIDE

Alan & Deborah Fowler

Sphere Reference

For Granny Scott – without whom nothing works

Sphere Reference
27 Wright's Lane
London W8 5SW

First published 1986

Copyright © 1986 Shepherd's Keep Studio Ltd

Typeset by The Word Factory Ltd, Rossendale, Lancs.
Printed and bound in Great Britain by

Acknowledgements

A great many people have helped us in the preparation of this book, and we would particularly like to thank: the Advertising Standards Authority; Aubrey Appleton, Distribution Services Ltd; Barclays Bank plc; Ted Daniels, IPC Magazines Ltd, Fred Hillier, Newspaper Publishers' Association; Hotchkiss Kruger Associates; the Independent Broadcasting Authority; Doreen Idle; John Keenan, PPA; John Liggett; Viola Niness; the Office of Fair Trading; Alan Pace, Overall Transport (UK) Ltd; the Post Office; Bob van Mook, Scotcade; and Ann Barrett for the illustrations.

Foreword

by Fred Hillier FICM,
Secretary of the National Newspapers Mail Order Protection Scheme

I was delighted when Alan and Debby Fowler approached me with their latest project, a book on starting a successful mail order business, and I am privileged to write these few words for them.

I have known Debby in a business capacity when she operated a mail order company some years ago; and I am well aware that she is highly qualified to write a work on the subject of a mail order business in general and on the advertising aspects in particular.

I cannot count the number of occasions in a year on which I am asked whether there is a standard book on starting a mail order business, which outlines the dangers, pitfalls and successes in equal parts.

To the best of my knowledge there is presently no such book and this excellent publication fills a much needed hole in the marketplace. It is full of common-sense advice about what the authors term 'the minefield' of mail order advertising. It deals in a very practical way with the subject in layman's terms but nevertheless makes the important points which can create a successful mail order business.

I beg you not to be put off by the many problems of running a mail order business but to remember that it is not a 'get rich quick' affair. Like any other business the rewards are commensurate to the energy, research and effort expended.

From my position in the mail order business I experience both the successes and failure of the industry and have always felt that many of its so-called disasters could have been avoided by taking prudent advice at an early stage.

If you are seriously considering operating a mail order business, whether it be as a first effort, or as a diversification of an existing business, I commend the common sense of this book to you.

Contents

Introduction

Look, the thing is, I've done it! Nearly ten years ago I started a mail order business with no money, no premises, no experience and a small baby to support. After a great deal of hard work, and backed by incredible help and support, I watched the business grow until it reached the dizzy heights of employing sixty people and producing a turnover of well over a million. But soon I also had to watch helplessly as the stock built to unmanageable proportions, the money ran out and customers' orders were fulfilled with increasing inefficiency. Finally, I saw 'my baby' taken over to be run by a larger and – this is the point – more professional concern, who also kindly gave me a job. Then, at last, far too late in the day, I learnt my trade.

I wish I had known then what I know now. It is not only my cry, but one I have heard on the lips of many people who have dabbled in the business. Mail order is all too often an industry into which people stumble for the wrong reasons, only to retire hurt, and considerably poorer, in a frighteningly short space of time. There is so little to read on the subject, yet, as a method of trading, it demands a great deal of understanding. It is for this reason in particular that Alan and I feel this book needs writing.

It *is* possible to build a mail order business which succeeds beyond your wildest dreams and, when it works, it has to be one of the most exciting and exhilarating of industries. But when it goes wrong, it goes wrong so fast you barely have time to realize what is happening before it is too late. It is the most volatile, the most fickle, the most unpredictable of businesses. Those who work in the industry, or on its fringes, can tell you stories of how fortunes are made and lost which you can scarcely believe, but which are more often than not quite true. Sometimes the simplest of ideas succeeds, where far more ambitious schemes have failed. There is no pattern, no secret formula to success.

However, there *is* a good solid living to be made – businesses can be built – and certainly after a difficult few years the potential for mail order growth is greater than it has been for some time. Response is stronger and better policing to prevent fraud has meant that public faith has been restored in the industry.

So on whatever level mail order attracts you, whether you have a product or a service to sell, please read on. Mail order is a minefield, but it is our intention to guide you through it.

Deborah Fowler

PART 1. IS YOUR IDEA VIABLE?

In the first section of this book, we are not actually telling you how to do *anything* – but please bear with us.

What we want to establish in these first three chapters is whether, in fact, the idea you have in mind is compatible with the mail order industry. We will be looking at the various different types of mail order business currently operating and getting a feel of what products tend to be best suited to this method of marketing.

By the end of the section, we hope you will have a greater degree of familiarity with the mail order trade and that ideas will be formulating in your mind as to how best you should be making your first approach to the market.

1.   Understanding the concept

What *is* mail order? It is largely a question of inspiring trust, of persuading your potential customers to purchase from you either your product or your service *sight unseen*. The customers may be presented with a beautiful colour brochure, an intriguing advertisement, a brilliant piece of descriptive copywriting, but, unlike shopping in the high street, they are unable to feel or touch the merchandise. They must make their judgement entirely on the information with which they are presented.

In general terms, this suggests that running a successful mail order business means that you are a slave to first-class marketing. You need to be able to identify and exploit those elements of what you have to offer which will have the maximum and widest appeal. It is also important to recognise that, by and large, mail order purchases are

impulse buys. Frequently, the mail order customer not only needs to be persuaded that your goods are of an acceptable price and quality, but also that he or she actually needs them at all. If that need has already been recognised, the chances are that what you are offering will have been purchased already through the normal retail channels.

Mail order comes in many guises, offering nowadays an astounding range of products in a very wide price bracket. You can buy a pair of sunglasses, a mink coat, a set of screwdrivers, a three-piece suite or a year's supply of disposable nappies. You can also learn to be a writer or organise your life insurance. The list appears endless, and yet it is readily recognised that, compared with most other Western countries, in Britain, we buy comparatively little in the way of mail order goods, which suggests there is enormous growth potential.

Whatever your trade, there are two main methods of selling by mail order, and it is important to understand the terminology – these methods are known as *direct mail* and *direct response advertising*. Let us look at these in turn.

DIRECT MAIL

Direct mail means just that – sending directly to your potential customers promotional literature describing what you have to sell and asking that they respond by placing orders. These days we are all bombarded with unsolicited literature through our letterboxes. Sometimes the letters are addressed to us personally (all too often, incorrectly!) and sometimes they are simply inserted with other mail. All this is *direct mail*. The supplier is forming a direct relationship with the customers, operating through no other media, agent or third party; it is a truly one-to-one relationship.

On the face of it, this seems like a marvellous idea. By cutting out the middle-men or -women, not only would it appear to be an enormous financial advantage (in theory both to you and your customers), but also it gives you the opportunity to put across the *exact* message you want your customer to receive. There can be few things more irritating than painstakingly working out your customers' precise requirements and then finding what you have to offer is being inexpertly, carelessly or even wrongly presented by agents, distributors or salesmen. Direct mail gives you control. You are in charge of your own destiny – provided, of course, you can present your product attractively enough to your customer.

DIRECT RESPONSE ADVERTISING

This is the placing of an advertisement in a newspaper, magazine, on television or radio, describing your wares and inviting potential customers to contact you with a view to placing an order. This particular method of selling by mail order sub-divides into two types.

1. Money-off-the-page advertising

This is where you invite your potential customer to order immediately. Having described your goods or services, with or without illustration, you invite the consumer to immediately place an order in response to your advertisement. The response is instantaneous. Your advertisement is read, watched or listened to, and, as a result, your potential customer may respond by sending you an order and usually payment.

2. Mail order advertising

This is where your advertisement invites the would-be customer to send for a catalogue or leaflet which will describe what you have to offer. This method of selling by mail order attracts a great deal less legislation than money-off-the-page advertising, as we will discuss in Chapter 4. However, it needs to be recognized that it does involve double promotional costs. Not only do you have to pay for the cost of the advertisement, but also for the cost of the brochure.

These, then, are the two main areas of mail order selling. Now let us look at the different types of mail order business which employ these methods.

THE BIG BOYS

Traditionally, mail order goods were sold via the big, flashy, colour catalogues, published twice a year. This method of selling has been employed for many years by the household names in mail order – Grattons, Littlewoods, Freemans, Empire Stores, etc. These catalogues are enormously expensive to produce and are dispatched biannually to 'agents'. The agent might be a person collating orders for an entire neighbourhood, but more often than not he or she is simply a person who buys a great deal of merchandise on behalf of friends and family from one particular catalogue.

These catalogues offer instalment credit terms, and without doubt are still the backbone of the mail order business in this country today. Yet it needs to be recognised that in the long term this method of selling could well become outdated. With the rise of new technology, perhaps a more exciting way of presenting goods could be through video or through a television information service, which enables you to dial into a catalogue on your own TV screen and place your order electronically. None the less, at the moment the big glossy catalogues still have a strong hold on the industry.

PARASITE MAIL ORDER

Here we are referring to those sectors of industry which provide a product or service totally unrelated to the mail order industry, on the back of which they run a mail order business. For a variety of reasons such businesses tend to be in regular correspondence with their customers and, since a postage stamp is required anyway, they feel they might as well use it as profitably as possible.

The most obvious example of this type of business is the credit card companies, who now have their own mail order catalogues which are mailed every so often with their customers' monthly statements. This also applies to such organisations as the Automobile Association and the Reader's Digest Association – indeed almost every organisation dealing direct with the consumer on a regular basis seems unable to resist the temptation to try to sell goods by mail order. One wonders how long it will be before our high street banks jump on the bandwagon!

HAVING IT BOTH WAYS

A number of retail outlets have realised the enormous value of mail order as a method of creating self-financing advertising. This equally applies the other way round. A number of mail order companies have seen how retail outlets can help expand their existing mail order business. At any rate, the idea of selling from selected shop premises as well as by mail order is an attractive one. Harrods, Habitat, Austin Reed, Laura Ashley are but a few examples which have proved enormously popular – and successful.

If you place a direct response advertisement in, for example, a Sunday supplement magazine, and it has been properly planned the response you will receive in terms of order value will make the whole exercise profitable in its own right. If at the same time you quote a list of your various shop branches, you will find that a number of people, in response to your advertisement, will go direct to your stores – perhaps for the very first time – in order to purchase what you are advertising. Once you have the customers in your stores, if your merchandise is appealing and your staff co-operative, you may well find that they buy considerably more goods than were promoted in your original advertisement. Even if the reader's response is entirely passive, the advertisement may have had the effect of imprinting in their mind the fact that there is a branch of your store locally which sells the type of merchandise displayed in the advertisement. When, at some time in the future, this merchandise is required, then the advertisement may well be recalled to mind.

Moreover, every customer who calls at your retail outlet should be either given, or provided with the opportunity to buy, a catalogue of your mail order goods. Properly handled, this makes the marketing both complementary and self-perpetuating.

MARKET STALL MAIL ORDER

This is where a company sets out to go into the mail order business quite specifically to sell a wide range of often totally unrelated goods. Just like the successful proprietor of a market stall, this type of mail order businessperson will study the market and decide what the consumer needs, and wants. Perhaps the most famous example of this is Scotcade, who have sold everything from silk shirts to kitchen equipment, furniture, garden tools and personalised Christmas goods. They approach their customers in two ways: they place a number of direct response advertisements, aiming carefully selected goods at particular magazines and newspapers. This not only sells their wares, but also attracts what they hope will be vital new blood to add to their existing list of customers. In addition, they produce a range of catalogues aimed at specific consumer profiles, which are mailed with a view to fulfilling that particular customer's needs. This type of business, then, is no more nor less than a retail outlet by mail. Just like your local village shopkeeper has to use skill in selecting the right goods to offer to the community, so, in the same way, the buyer for this type of mail order catalogue will select any merchandise which he or she feels will be suitable for the growing list of customers.

MAKING FOR MAIL ORDER

One of the most successful entrées into the mail order market in recent years has been made by existing manufacturers. Take a company which has built up a successful manufacturing business, very often supplying major mail order companies. As the business grows, it becomes increasingly attractive to go into mail order direct – thus cutting out the middle-man or -woman. This can work very well, since obviously the manufacturer has a good background knowledge of what sells – not only in terms of type of merchandise, but also details, such as sizes and colours, where appropriate. Sometimes the manufacturer may be understandably worried about upsetting existing customers with the establishment of a new business, but this problem can be overcome by the use of a fulfilment house, as we will discuss in detail in Chapter 16. Suffice it to say here that if you are a manufacturer successfully selling your merchandise to an established mail order company, if you want to build your own business you are probably very well placed to do so, provided you have the right help.

CLUBBING TOGETHER

Book clubs, of course, are the major contributor in this field, although tapes and records are sold by this method too. To join a club customers are usually offered a book or record at an incredibly knocked-down price, in return for which they guarantee to buy a minimum of four or five items during the rest of the year. Thereafter, each month they are supplied with a list from which to choose.

The marketing pitch of a club is not simply to provide a range of goods. Quite specifically, the aim is to offer their members items at below the normal retail price. In addition, there is the suggestion that the selection process had weeded out for their members the very best of what is on offer – they are supplying a service too. In other words, avid readers, instead of having to scour the bestselling lists or read book reviews, simply rely on the club to point them in the direction of the best books available on the market. Clubs have been through a difficult period, but like the rest of the mail order industry things are improving greatly and the future looks very bright indeed.

PART WORKS

This method of selling by mail order has been in existence for a long time. Normally it is associated with major publishers, who, over a period, invite subscriptions for, say, a month-by-month cookery or car maintenance course. This concept has now expanded into other fields. For example, parents can buy for their pre-school children an early learning course, where on the payment of an initial sum a progressive package of books and playthings are dispatched automatically each month. This can work very well, though consistency in terms of quality of what is supplied is vitally important.

One of the earliest advocates of part works was Charles Dickens, who sold many of his classic stories by this method, on an instalment basis.

Will Oliver be given some more? Read next week's instalment.

SERVICE WITH A STAMP

A number of service industries have built up very successful mail order businesses. Insurance companies have discovered that one of the most effective ways of selling life insurance is by mail order. Financial consultants in a range of fields have found that they can offer their services in this way, too. And then there is the large established market of adult education. Indeed, it is possible these days to buy a course through mail order from which you can learn to do almost *anything*!

GENERAL BUSINESS INDUSTRIAL DIRECT MAIL

When one thinks of mail order, there is a tendency to view the industry as a service to the consumer. However, as already indicated, there is considerable scope in the business/industrial sector. These days, putting a decent salesman on the road, plus car, is going to cost between fifteen and twenty thousand pounds, and that sort of money will buy an awful lot of advertising. The beauty of industrial mail order is that, usually – unlike selling to the domestic consumer – the customer is obvious, so that any mail shot can be targeted precisely to the people who will be most interested in what you have to offer. The same applies to advertising, since almost certainly you will be able to advertise in trade magazines, where the reader is already categorised as a potential customer by virtue of the fact that he or she subscribes to the magazine.

A growing number of companies now use mail order as a back-up to their existing sales force, or, in some instances, instead of one. We feel there is great growth potential in this area.

So the mail order market can be approached in many ways, and perhaps now, more than at any other time, there are immense opportunities for development, provided you approach the whole concept with extreme respect and caution. The wide use of credit cards, of course, has greatly facilitated armchair shopping. The constant improvement in computers, both for mailing, order processing and the forecasting of order response, has helped to stabilise and improve the efficiency of the industry. With the problems of parking, traffic and the cost of petrol balanced against a future of cable and satellite television, video recorders and facilities such as Ceefax, the attractions of taking the hassle out of shopping by doing it all from home have to be enormous.

The future for mail order looks bright. Let us see if there is a place in it for you and your business.

2. Selecting the right product

Traditionally, when one thinks of mail order one tends to think of the fashion trade, since in the past fashion has provided the backbone to the industry. Not any more: as we have already indicated, in theory at any rate, one can sell absolutely anything by mail order.

There are six major factors which will affect whether your product or service will sell by mail order. These are as follows:

Price
Quality
Presentation
Uniqueness of design
Availability
Transport

Let us look at these points one by one.

PRICE

Because a mail order purchase represents a direct relationship between supplier and customer, the tendency in the past has been to believe that goods sold by mail order must be cheap. This is not the case. In fact, the industry is not nearly as price sensitive as one might imagine. Certainly these days it is possible to sell high-value items by mail order and, in trying to evaluate a price structure, you should be thinking more in terms of providing value for money, rather than a bargain. Of course, some very successful businesses have been built on the basis of offering items which can be seen to be selling at considerably less than normal market price, but this is by no means the only way of selling by mail order.

The price you can charge, to a large extent, will be influenced by other factors, such as the uniqueness and quality of the product, and the ease with which your customer can obtain such goods elsewhere. By way of an example, some years ago we were tremendously success-ful in selling – both by catalogue and through newspaper advertisements – a basic, navy blue, cotton fisherman's smock for both adults and children. We manufactured these ourselves and could not begin to compete in price with those being offered in the chandlery shops around our coasts. But it did not matter. We were offering something that, unless you happened to live near a coastal resort, you simply could not buy anywhere else.

In deciding whether your product or service is suitable for mail order, quite clearly the first consideration must be price. As a basic rule, we would suggest that if you are selling an item which is to retail at less than £75 per unit, you should take the basic cost of that item, multiply it by three and add on VAT, where applicable, in order to reach your correct selling price. This applies whether you are selling that item through your own brochure or through a direct response advertisement.

We recognise that in some instances it may not be possible to obtain such a high gross margin and on items selling for over £75 it is probably not essential for profitability. This brings us on to the question of unit cost. If you are selling your goods through your own catalogue, then it is important that you display a good range of prices, so however small the spending power of your potential customers, there is something to suit them. If you are selling an item from a direct response *colour* advertisement, we do not believe that your unit selling price should be less than £20, and, in the case of a *black and white* classified advertisement, not less than £5. This has to be a generalisation, of course, but we would recommend that you look on our suggestions as more of a rule than a yardstick. Whatever the size of your gross profit percentage, you must recognise the enormous costs involved in both advertising and administering the sale of goods by mail order. If your unit selling price is too low, there is just not enough cash available to meet those costs.

A word on postage and packing. It is normal in most mail order advertising to quote postage and packing as a separate figure. We would suggest that your basic cost of packing, for instance, the presentation box or whatever, should be included as part of your unit cost before you add on your gross profit. Therefore the postage and packing figure shown on the advertisement, or on your catalogue order form, should largely relate to the cost of postage. If your postage and packing charges are too high, this tends to upset the customers.

Another very important factor which should affect your attitude to pricing regards the rate of returns. If you are intending to sell fashion by mail order, you must be prepared for up to 25 per cent of everything you send out to come back. However carefully you detail the measurement chart as a guideline to your customers, there are extraneous factors which you cannot control. Customers may return a garment because it does not suit them, or because the fabric or colour is not what they expected. Then there is the self-delusion factor: women, in particular, have a tendency to order the size they like to think of themselves as being. If a woman is determined she is a size 14, even though she needs a size 16, nine times out of ten she will order a size 14, only to have to send it back for a larger size – complaining, of course, that your sizing is too skimpy.

It is not purely fashion that suffers from returns, of course, and until you have had some experience selling your product it will be very difficult to gauge the reject rate. However, we would recommend that you allow 25 per cent return rate for fashion items and 10 per cent for non-fashion items.

Case history

Pat, a great friend of ours, ordered by mail order a set of French cooking pots and casserole dishes a few months ago. When she received them she was very impressed by their quality, but she decided that they were far too heavy and cumbersome to deal with on a day-to-day basis. She therefore decided to return them to the supplier. Having repacked them with great difficulty, Pat lugged them down to the post office – nearly doing herself a mischief in the process – only to be told that the parcel was too heavy for the post office to handle and that clearly the goods had been dispatched to her originally by carrier. An hour later, almost on hands and knees, she dragged the enormous parcel back home again and after a few frantic phone calls found a carrier to pick it up for her.

A few days later, a very pleasant man from the supplier telephoned to inquire the cost of her returning the parcel so that he could include this in the refund cheque. In passing he said how sorry he was that she had not been pleased with the goods and that he had been very surprised to receive them back, since hers was the first order that had ever been returned. As she said to us, she was not at all surprised!

Certainly, the more difficult it is to return goods, the more likely they are to be retained, and there is also the inertia factor: even if the goods are not right, people quite often cannot be bothered to return them. However, we would not suggest that you calculate your return rate on this basis. What you should be doing is to provide goods consistent in quality with what you have led your customers to expect – that is the best way to avoid returns.

QUALITY

There are many wide-ranging views on the subject of mail order quality and what you have to do first is to decide the nature of your mail order business. Are you trying to build a long-term business with regular customers, who will provide, in time, a good, solid sales base? If so, cutting corners on quality will not pay off in the long term. The question you have to ask yourself is whether you want your customers to order from you again, or whether you are content to take their money once only.

Of course selling by mail order enables you to cheat. I (Deborah) some time ago had a long argument with a merchandising manager concerning a design of mine. He insisted that the pockets on the jacket I had made could be left off because they would not show up in the photograph. Have you ever tried wearing a jacket without pockets? It is awful! I have to admit I was secretly pleased when, having lost the argument, the returns on the jacket were considerable.

We would like to stress that if the quality of your goods does not

match up to your claims in the advertisement, you are building yourself a load of headaches, which may well bring your business to its knees. Servicing dissatisfied customers by mail is far more difficult than through a normal retail outlet. Once customers return their goods, they are angry and disappointed and they expect replacements or a refund by return. By law, you must refund not only the cost of the goods, but the cost of postage. Add on the administration time and the fact that the goods may not be able to be resold and you really are looking at a very expensive business. Not only that, you have lost a customer; when you consider how much it has cost you to reach that customer in the first place, it is something you simply cannot afford to do.

Case history

A year or so ago, we were visiting a well-known dress manufacturer who has worked for the mail order trade for many years and who has a unique understanding of the business. He was supplying a dress as a special offer in one of the major women's magazines. The magazine had just arrived on his desk. Rows of dresses stood out in his workshop ready to be dispatched. When we were shown into his office, we found him with his head in his hands, full of gloom.

'What's wrong, Charlie?' we asked.

'Look at this, just look at this.' He spun the magazine for us to see. It was a sensational advertisement, beautifully photographed. It was autumn and they were selling a Christmas party dress – the woman looked elegant, sophisticated, slim and poised.

We stared at him, uncomprehendingly. 'So, what's wrong with this?' we asked.

'It's much too good,' Charlie said. 'That bloody photographer, see how he has lit the dress. He's been careful not to bounce the light off the sheen of the polyester. That dress looks a million dollars. Come outside and I'll show you the real thing.'

It was a pleasant enough little polyester dress, but we saw what he meant immediately. It in no way related to the stylish design in the magazine 'We'll have thousands back,' he said, 'thousands!' And he did.

PRESENTATION

A lesson in presentation can be learnt from the case history quoted above. On a mundane level, presentation is giving the customer the right information about what you have to offer in the most attractive way possible. The illustration or photograph, of course, is very important, but so is the copy. The clever use of words can make all the difference to the success or failure of your advertising. In Chapters 7 and 8 we will be discussing in detail how best to put together an advertisement and a brochure. Suffice it to say here that clever presentation can drastically affect the price you can charge – but that is only half the story.

Presentation of the goods, when they arrive at the customer's front door, is also vitally important. Good packaging is essential, not just for safety reasons, but so that the items arrive looking good. Before you settle on any particular type of packaging, you ought to try sending yourself some of your own goods and see if they live up to your expectations on arrival.

Presentation is not simply a question of showing off the product to best advantage either. It should be doing more. You should be trying to project a lifestyle. The customer should react to the illustration by thinking, I would like to do that, look like that . . . or whatever. You should be telling a story.

You also have to consider the long-term image of your business. Image-building can be done in so many ways. For example, a well-known clothing manufacturers' hallmark is the use of non-professional models. This gives their catalogue a cosy, laid-back, homely feel, which is instantly recognisable. This sort of image building is of enormous value.

Television presentation

While on the subject of presentation, it is sensible to discuss TV direct response advertising. At the moment, this is still pretty much in its infancy. Undoubtedly, if you have a product which you think could be sold via a TV advertisement you will find that television companies are very receptive to doing a deal, since they are anxious to develop this form of advertising. However, experience suggests that the only type of direct response advertisements which really work are those selling records or tapes – in other words, sound-related items. The reason for this, we believe, is because the advertisement needs to make an other than visual impact on the potential customer.

What do we mean? Well, most families are the same: when the advertisements come on, mother puts on the kettle, father gets another beer, or whatever. Generally, the family is on the move. The same music being constantly repeated, with instructions on how to order it, can have an impact on the family, even while they are doing other things. This would not be the case if you were trying to sell a dress, a saucepan, or a garden mower. So, if you are considering the possibility of selling your goods via television, bear in mind that your presentation needs to work without any visual contact with your customer.

UNIQUENESS

Your product or service does not need to be unique in order to be sold by mail order . . . but it helps. Obviously if there is no immediately comparable item available for purchase, then what you have to offer has to be less price sensitive. As we saw with the fishermen's smocks, because they were garments that could not be bought in the average high street shop, they sold well.

Alternatively, there are certain items which are ageless and which can continue to sell by mail order year after year, with perhaps a few concessions to the changing world by the introduction of a different colour or a slight alteration in style. If you want to find a regular bread-and-butter-line, we would suggest that you consult a number of current newspapers and magazines and then buy back copies of the same publications of, say, two or three years ago. Compare the advertisements, especially those belonging to the same company, and see how the items they have to sell have changed. You can bet your life there is no way someone is going to go on running an advertisement that does not work.

Surprisingly ordinary items sell very well, and time spent studying other people's advertisements, and sending for other company's brochures, is well worth while. Study, too, consecutive brochures belonging to the same company and see which items they have carried forward into the new brochure – these are the winners. Study the price, the presentation, the quality of the item, and see how it compares with what you have to offer. You do not have to be unique, you do not even have to be better, *but you do have to be as good*.

AVAILABILITY

This is the cornerstone of every successful mail order business. If you cannot react to demand, then you cannot go into mail order. It is as simple as that. If you are a manufacturer, can you cope with unprecedented demand if your advertisement or catalogue is very successful? Equally important, have you a way of disposing of your surplus stock through another source if your efforts in mail order fail?

If you are buying in your goods, you have to be very careful. You need to tie down your suppliers to very specific delivery guarantees, which, inevitably, they will try to wriggle out of. However, you cannot take the risk of being let down. Having committed yourself to a large advertising expenditure, you must not put yourself in the position where you cannot fulfil orders.

Of course the most vulnerable area of supply is imported goods. We have all been on holiday and seen items on display which we know are being sold at a fraction of what they would cost in England. It is tempting to think, for example, that you could bring leather belts into this country for twenty pence each, and sell them for five pounds. In practice it is not so easy. To secure a large enough stock to cope with the maximum possible demand usually means an enormous capital outlay; anything less runs the risk of unfulfilled orders. Many mail order companies rely very heavily on imports, particularly in the fashion business, but this kind of trading can produce horrendous ulcers. Mention the words 'dock strike' or 'quotas' to the average mail order person trading in this way and he or she will have a severe fit of palpitations. If you must import, find a really reliable supplier, deal direct with the manufacturer – not a middle-man or -woman – and get yourself an efficient freight forwarder.

So the message is this: make sure that you can respond to demand, whatever that demand may be, and make sure, too, that you can dispose of your stock if your promotions do not work well.

TRANSPORT

In Chapter 14 we deal in detail with the various schemes available from the Post Office and its competitors with regard to the transport of your mail order goods. Without a doubt, transport facilities in this country have improved enormously and there is plenty of variety to choose from. However, if you require the facility of having individual parcels delivered all over the country, any service other than the Post Office is going to prove expensive. Therefore the weight factor of your goods needs to be very carefully considered. It is crucial to your costs.

Consider very carefully too your packaging. Packaging is very expensive, but never more so than when it is inadequate. Make sure your goods can be transported safely and delivered promptly.

So in assessing whether your goods or services are suitable for mail order, you have to consider all these points, not only individually, but in relation to one another. Having done that, you must compare what you have to offer with the marketplace as a whole.

3.   Identifying the market

Let us assume for the moment that you have decided what product, or range of products, you are going to sell by mail order. Before you can take the idea any further, it is very important that you first identify who it is you imagine is going to respond to your advertising.

Let us look at some facts. The largest target group to buy from mail order is women between the ages of forty-five and sixty. The next, and you may find this surprising, is young people between the ages of seventeen and twenty-two – largely, one imagines, because they have the highest amount of disposable income. Clearly, therefore, if your product or service can be aimed at one of these groups, it has to be a major advantage.

However, do not immediately panic here and throw away your idea because it does not seem to conform to these two main target areas. Apart from any other consideration, you may find that in fact it does! Take, for instance, the lawn-mower you are selling. Certainly, in your early advertisements you need to experiment with different models to see whether you can obtain a better result having a woman pushing it, rather than a man, which may well be the case. Select your female model particularly carefully. In this instance, she should be attractive, but not too young. In other words, the models you use will greatly influence the range of appeal.

Having looked, in a broad sense, at the most receptive people, let us now see where they live. Here is a list of regional markets in order of highest response rate:

Wales;
The South-west;
Scotland and the north of England;
London and the Home Counties (London and the Home Counties have proved to be a very poor fourth – way behind the others in terms of response).

Of course, this information is of the most help when it comes to selecting regional advertising, but nevertheless we felt it relevant to quote here, since if you know where most of your customers are likely to live, it may influence how you present your advertising.

As your business develops, it naturally becomes a great deal easier to identify your customer, but you must never become too complacent – there are often some surprises in store. We used to be associated with a company who sold fashion aimed specifically at the older woman. Shortly before Christmas they included in their catalogue a thermal balaclava helmet – hardly, you would think, the most scintillating fashion item. The response was incredible; they sold thirty-three thousand in less than a fortnight and such was the phenomenal response they felt they had to find out who was buying them. Was every little old lady in the country dashing around in a balaclava?

A series of tactful inquiries to their most regular customers soon solved the mystery. It was a cold winter and the balaclavas were being bought for husbands, sons and grandsons to wear under their crash helmets when riding motorcycles. Our colleagues used their initiative and reacted immediately. They quickly brought out a catalogue of motorcycle accessories and mailed them to everyone who had ordered a balaclava helmet. The response was again astounding; they had pitched right into a ready-made market. Suddenly, a company, which up until then had been solely involved in supplying the older woman, had a brand new business on its hands.

So far in this chapter we have been talking about general consumer items and it may be that, in your case, your buyer is already clearly defined, simply by the very nature of the product or service you are offering. For example, supposing you are intending to sell fishing tackle by mail order. Clearly you are only interested in contacting the nation's fishermen and promoting your products may be best served by advertising exclusively in specialist magazines and sending out your brochure to members of fishing clubs. Even here, however, we would suggest that you need to know what age group and sex is predominantly responding to your advertisements. If you find it is the older age group, then perhaps you may want to slightly change the emphasis of your product range – perhaps including a comfortable fishing stool or a range of protective clothing. On the face of it, this may seem rather facile, but then marketing is only really a question of common sense. Recognise who your customer is and tailor make your approach to suit him or her.

The secret of survival in mail order is to test and keep testing and, above all, to learn from those tests. All through this book you will find that we preach caution, suggesting that you should not invest in a large advertising programme until you have first established that there is a market for what you have to offer. Nevertheless there is no point in undermining your chances of success by economising to the point where you cannot be possibly reaching the right people. For example, our experience suggests that it is not usually possible to establish a mail order business by advertising in your local newspapers. On the face of it, this might seem the most economic and safe course of action, but it simply will not work. Strangely enough, with our business we found that having established a national reputation by advertising in Sunday supplement magazines, small advertisements in the local press, for specific reasons such as special or bargain offers, worked well – but only when we first established a national name. By the same token, there is no point in advertising in a small circulation, down-market magazine when your customer profile suggests you should be advertising in the *Sunday Times* magazine supplement.

What you have to do is to establish the best possible method of reaching the people most likely to purchase from you. If you are intending to employ direct response advertising, in Chapter 5 of this book you will find a comprehensive list of newspapers and magazines. Study this list and, having selected what you consider to be the most suitable publications for your use, buy copies of them all and look carefully at the advertisements. Be highly suspicious where a magazine carries very few advertisements. This usually means that, although the magazine may be splendid editorially, it does not have good advertising pulling power. By contrast, in other magazines, do not be dismayed at the amount of competition you may see from existing advertisers – this simply means you have selected the right media. Remember our doctrine in the previous chapter: you do not have to be *better*, you just need to be *as good*.

When it comes to mailing a brochure, again the last thing you want to do is to mail it at random. The cost of sending out a brochure is very high and it would be the height of folly to send it to somebody who is entirely unsuitable. Building a list yourself is a painstaking business. It means placing advertisements – either direct response or small classified advertisements aimed at advertising your brochure – and compiling a list of names from the responses you receive. In time the replies must be sifted into two groups – those who order and those who do not. This is vital information for future mailings. (There is a whole raft of people who send for every available brochure advertised and never order a thing!)

There are shortcuts to this procedure. There are a number of list brokers about, who sell mailing lists on behalf of other mail order companies. The normal procedure is that for a price – usually somewhere between £25 and £60 per thousand names – you can buy in a list of names which you may use once only. Those people, however, who actually order from you direct as a result of your mailing shot become your property and you may continue to mail them in the future. The rest must never be used again. A list broker normally has a catalogue showing the companies whose lists he can rent on your behalf. On the face of it, if you are, for instance, setting up a children's book club, renting the Mothercare list would appear to be an excellent idea. However, we do not advocate this method.

Think about it for a moment. If you had painstakingly built up a list of names of people who ordered regularly and well from you, would you dream of passing that list on to anyone else, even if their products were not the same as yours? No, of course you would not. If you were successfully selling, for example, blankets, duvets, sheets and towels to a successful list of people, you would be worried sick if you exposed them to a company selling kitchenware. You would be concerned lest your precious customers started spending more money on their kitchens than they had hitherto been spending on their bedrooms and bathrooms.

So where does that leave the list brokers? What it essentially means is that mail order companies only release those names which are proving to be of little or no use to themselves. We know this is not what list brokers' catalogues usually say. Extravagant claims are made about supplying only proven buyers, but what they do not tell you is how long ago the customer ordered, or how much he or she spent. On the whole, list brokers trade in second-class names – and do you want your brochure to go out in those circumstances?

The alternative to the list broker is to deal direct with a specialist group of people. We mentioned earlier fishing clubs in relation to selling fishing tackle and this is the kind of approach you could make. A number of large organisations are often quite willing to rent out their names direct to a mail order company, once they have satisfied themselves that the product or service you intend to offer is a bona fide one. A word of caution here, though: whilst people belonging to a fishing club need fishing tackle, they are not necessarily mail order buyers. In fairness to the list brokers, at some time the people on their lists have shown an interest in mail order. There is a whole sector of the population who, under no circumstances, will ever order anything through the post. As a method of shopping, it simply does not appeal. In approaching a specialist list, therefore, you must recognise this phenomena and be cautious – they may buy fishing tackle, but not by mail order.

We have stressed the need to test, but it is such an important point that we think it bears repeating. In your search for your potential customer, do not get hoodwinked into committing yourself to a long-term advertising programme until you have thoroughly tested the market. Do not book several advertisements in a single magazine until you have seen the results of the first one. Do not buy in fifty thousand names – ask for a sample thousand to test first.

In conclusion, decide upon the market you consider to be most suitable for what you have to offer. Then, tailor make your product or service to suit that market. This may not mean altering your product as such, but simply presenting it in the most effective way for your potential customer. Having satisfied yourself on these points, you must then look at the most reliable and cost effective way of reaching that market. In the next section of this book, we will tell you how best to do just that.

PART 2. SETTING OUT YOUR STALL

This section is a step-by-step guide on how to start mail order advertising for the first time. It covers both newspaper and magazine advertising and the production and distribution of your own brochure. By the end of the section you will know how, and where, you are going to advertise initially and the implications of doing so.

Selling goods by mail is now the subject of stringent controls – and rightly so. You cannot simply telephone a newspaper or magazine and place a money-off-the-page advertisement without being vetted carefully first. Even the publication of your own brochure is subject to a code of practice. It is very important that you are aware of these regulations, for the protection not only of your potential customer but yourself.

Obviously, mail order advertising is not simply a question of applying the right rules. The way in which you display your advertisements will greatly influence their chances of success; how your goods are presented in a brochure is vital. In this section we will be covering these areas in detail.

So you believe you have selected the right product and you know the market at which you are aiming. Then let us pursue it.

4. Advertising legislation

Because mail order customers are buying goods on trust – in most cases actually parting with their money before they can see and touch what they have bought – it is necessary for there to be fairly tight legislation in order to protect their interests. The Office of Fair Trading have laid down very careful guidelines as to how mail order transactions should be operated.

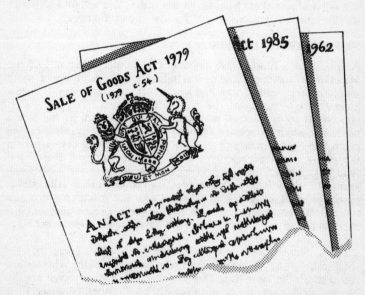

As a result of this, a number of trade associations have introduced the Mail Order Protection Scheme (MOPS) geared to protect newspaper and magazine readers responding to money-off-the-page advertisements. There are five MOP schemes: the Newspaper Publishers' Association cover national newspapers, the Newspaper Society represents local newspapers, the Periodical Publishers' Association, magazines, and two Scottish schemes, the Scottish Newspaper Proprietors' Association and the Scottish Daily Newspaper Society. A similar scheme is run by the Independent Broadcasting Authority to protect commercial radio and television advertising. In addition, the Mail Order Publishers' Association have a code of practice which lays down rules for its members concerning purchases from catalogues or brochures. Add to this the fact that all advertisements must conform to the Advertising Standards Authority guidelines and you can see that you have to be very careful indeed how you trade.

We thought it would be helpful if we broke down this legislation into a series of manageable headings, which are as follows:

Newspaper advertising
Magazine advertising
Advertising on television and radio
Catalogues and brochures
Advertising Standards Authority
Summary of customers' rights

We will deal with these headings in that order. You will find addresses for the various organisations listed at the end of the book.

NEWSPAPER ADVERTISING

As a result of a considerable amount of mail order abuse, in 1975 the Mail Order Protection Scheme was initiated, the specific aim of which was to protect readers who had lost money as a direct result of responding to a money-off-the-page advertisement. The scheme is policed, as far as national newspapers are concerned, by the Newspaper Publishers' Association (NPA) who are also responsible for the control and maintenance of a central fund to which all newspapers in the scheme contribute and from which all claims are paid. The central fund is supported by fees paid by both advertisers and advertising agents, in addition to the newspapers' own contributions. All national newspapers subscribe to this scheme, with the result that it is not theoretically possible to place a money-off-the-page advertisement in a national newspaper without having first made application to the NPA for approval to advertise.

For a detailed look at the MOP scheme we are going to refer specifically to the NPA for ease of reference, but all the schemes are run in much the same way. The other organisations involved are the Newspaper Society, the Scottish Newspaper Proprietors' Association and the Scottish Daily Newspaper Society.

When you contact the NPA, they will send you full details of their Mail Order Protection Scheme, together with application forms. These forms are relatively simple to complete and should be returned together with the appropriate fee. Fees are calculated on a sliding scale and are currently at £60 for an annual advertising expenditure of under £5,000, escalating to £1,000 for an advertising expenditure of over £300,000.

Advertising is every newspaper's bread and butter, but, as far as

money-off-the-page advertising is concerned, they have to be very ca[...]
indeed whom they accept, for obvious reasons. In order to be accepted by
the NPA, you will have to demonstrate that you have a financially sound
business – which means that if you have been trading for some time, you
must be trading profitably, and if you are a new company, that you have a
very strong capital base. The NPA will be interested also in your management structure and are more likely to accept your application if you
have in your employ experienced mail order personnel.

On receipt of your application, the procedure is as follows. The NPA will
pursue the normal credit inquiries, take up trade and bank references, and
then their representative may visit your premises. As a result of these
inquiries the NPA will react in one of three ways:

1. If they are not happy with your business in its current circumstances,
   they will send you a letter inviting you to make an application again
   on a later date. In the meantime, they will suggest that you should
   gain some mail order experience. This, of course, puts you into a
   'chicken and egg' situation. How can you gain experience without
   being able to advertise? What they are saying is that you should
   concentrate on advertising in lower circulation newspapers, or
   magazines, where your application to advertise may be more
   acceptable. Alternatively, you can build up sales through brochure
   distribution.
2. They may accept your application but look for some additional
   financial back-up to protect your customers. This could take one of
   the following forms:
   (a) a bank guarantee – anything from £2,000 to £100,000;
   (b) an insurance bond – where payment of an annual premium
       would provide insurance cover for an agreed amount, so that
       there would be independent funds available to satisfy the claims
       of customers in the event of your business failing;
   (c) parent company guarantee – if you are a wholly owned sub-
       sidiary of a publicly quoted company;
   (d) stake holder's account – where a professional person, for ex-
       ample, a solicitor or an accountant, receives all the money
       generated from your advertisements and only releases it to you
       when he or she is satisfied that goods have been dispatched to
       the customers (this arrangement is not proving very satisfactory
       as it is expensive and difficult to administer and few people,
       therefore, want to take on the responsibility).
3. If your application is successful, but the NPA consider you may not
   be able to cope with substantial volumes of trade, you may be given
   conditional approval, for example, there may be restrictions on the
   price of the product you are aiming to sell, or on the amount of your
   advertising expenditure.
4. The NPA may also suggest that where response volumes are high, a
   fulfilment house should be employed. A fulfilment house is an
   organisation which will hold an advertiser's stock, receive the

pack and dispatch them and, after deducting their hand-
arge, rebate the remainder to the advertiser. In order to
ly with the Mail Order Transactions (Information) Order
, the advertisement must appear in the name of the
filment house. That said, however, the true advertiser's
ddress may appear outside the coupon, but the address of the
fulfilment house must appear inside the coupon.

Once you have NPA approval, you may display the MOPS logo on
all your money-off-the-page advertisements, which, of course, gives
immediate reassurance to the potential customer. However, this logo

applies to the NPA only and may not be used on your brochures, nor
on any classified advertisement, nor in any other media such as
magazines, local press or television.

The MOPS scheme comes into operation in the case of the
advertiser's bankruptcy, liquidation, or where he or she has ceased to
trade. In these circumstances, the central fund will repay all customers
who have lost money as a direct result of responding to newspaper
money-off-the-page advertisements. Those claims from customers,
who originally paid for goods by credit card, are treated in a slightly
different way. Where the sum is over £100, credit card companies are
entirely liable for the refund. Where the amount is under £100, the
credit card company still makes the refund for simplicity of
administration, but they can then claim the money back from the NPA.
It is worth making the point here that only Access and Barclaycard are
considered as actual credit cards. Diners Club and American Express
are not and payments made through these cards are the full responsibility of the NPA when it comes to refund.

In previous chapters we have suggested that almost anything can be
sold by mail order, but it is worth mentioning that the following items
will not be covered by MOPS and therefore cannot be sold via
money-off-the-page advertising:

> foodstuffs of any description;
> contraceptives or kindred products – though these may be
> advertised in the classified section under 'Personal';
> any product which appeals to fear or superstition, such as lucky
> charms or horoscopes.

Having read this section, you may feel that your financial situation will not stand up to NPA scrutiny and that you will not be able to give them the reassurance of a bank guarantee, nor afford to pay an expensive insurance premium. However, this need not necessarily preclude you from advertising in national newspapers, and these are the circumstances in which you can advertise without prior NPA approval:

1. You may invite readers to send for a catalogue or brochure, giving details of your product. The brochure can be supplied free, or at a price of £1 or less. Sales resulting from your brochures and catalogues clearly will not be protected by the MOPS central fund.

2. You may invite readers to visit your retail premises to purchase the goods you are advertising.

2. You may offer a service – such as membership of a club, magazine subscriptions, film processing, ordering of theatre tickets – without NPA approval. However, you must be careful not to form any direct purchasing relationship. For example, if a replacement film can be purchased and added to the film processing charge, that would represent money-off-the-page advertising and therefore would need approval.

4. You can advertise without prior approval under a newspaper's classified section, such as 'Personal', 'Motoring', 'House and Garden', etc.

5. You can advertise goods which are being sent on approval, or for cash on delivery, or in any circumstances where, initially, the reader is only required to pay a small remittance to cover carriage costs.

6. You can advertise goods which can only be purchased when coupons from products obtained through retail outlets are included in the order.

7. You can sell any item costing 25p or less.

Certainly, our advice would be that if you are a new company starting out in mail order for the first time, you might well be advised to begin by placing classified advertisements for your brochure in a variety of newspapers to test their response. This will build up your experience and confidence. It will show you which newspapers respond best to your particular product and it will also demonstrate to the NPA, when you come to make you application, that you have acquired a degree of mail order experience.

MAGAZINE ADVERTISING

The major magazine groups are covered by the Periodical Publishers' Association (PPA). The PPA operate in a similar way to the NPA, except that they have no central MOPS organisation or fund. Advertisers have a direct relationship with individual magazines, each of which is responsible for safeguarding the readers' interests and making refunds where they are let down.

Details and application forms for direct response advertising can be obtained from the PPA, or from the magazine in which you intend to advertise.

All of the comments made under the heading of newspaper advertising apply also to magazine advertising. However, on the whole it is slightly easier to be accepted by the PPA member magazines than by the NPA. This is for very obvious reasons, since the power of advertising is much greater within the newspaper groups because of their enormous circulation. A magazine is doing very well indeed if it has a circulation of fifty thousand, whereas a national newspaper can expect a circulation of well over a million.

ADVERTISING ON TELEVISION AND RADIO

Advertising on television and radio has to conform with specific standards in much the same way as newspapers and magazines. The body controlling these standards is the Independent Broadcasting Authority (IBA).

The major difference between the IBA and the NPA/PPA is that the standards laid down for radio and TV advertising are governed by statute – in other words, they are legal requirements. The current legislation was introduced by the Broadcasting Act of 1981, which defines what is known as *essential duties and responsibilities*. Unlike magazine and newspaper advertising, every TV advertisement is pre-vetted twice by IBA executives before it is allowed to be broadcast. This ensures that every broadcast advertisement is approved *before* it goes out. This contrasts with the printed advertisement, which ought to conform to advertising standards but sometimes does not, since the vetting process is restricted to the harassed advertising manager at each publication.

The other main difference is that *all* screen direct response advertising has to be operated through a stake-holder or trust fund account. In other words, all monies received from such advertising must be handled by an appointed stake-holder – an accountant, solicitor or banker – who must satisfy himself or herself that the goods have been dispatched satisfactorily before releasing the money to the advertiser.

Undoubtedly there are some good deals to be had in booking TV direct response advertising. Most independent television companies are prepared to offer very low advertising rates in exchange for some sort of profit share deal with the advertiser. Naturally this greatly reduces the risk factor, but it is still quite possible to loose a substantial amount of money, since this form of advertising is still rather a hit and miss affair and production costs can be very high.

It also should be noted that direct response advertising, booked on a profit share basis, is not allowed to be screened between 6 p.m. and 10 p.m. (peak viewing time).

As we have already discussed in the first section of this book, direct response TV advertising is a very dangerous game and clearly it would appear that no one has made much money out of the exercise to date, with the possible exception of record companies. We have talked to several television stations and, reading between the lines, we get the impression that direct response advertising is certainly not a growth area at present, which suggests that a number of advertisers have retired hurt. You may feel that you are the pioneer who can change everything, but if this is your attitude we would ask you to heed our advice: *do construct an advertisement which stands up on its own aurally as well as visually*.

The television companies have combined to form the Independent Television Companies Association (ITCA). The ITCA have a *Direct Response Advertising Subcommittee*, who have established specific rules and regulations for direct response advertising. It would be well worth while writing to them and asking for a copy of these rules.

As far as radio is concerned, no one has attempted direct response advertising in this media to any large degree. If you were to operate such a scheme, your advertising would be covered by the same IBA rules as for television. You might receive some response from inviting listeners to apply for your brochure, but, on the whole, radio stations are best used for the advertising of local retail outlets.

CATALOGUES, BROCHURES AND LEAFLETS

The publishing of your own catalogue is not subject to the same degree of legislation as direct response advertising. Nevertheless, failure to comply with the code of practice laid down for mail order trading could land you in trouble with the Office of Fair Trading, or the Advertising Standards Authority, or you could be taken to court and be successfully sued by one or more customers, possibly through the involvement of your local trading standards officer. We would suggest that you write to the British Direct Marketing Association and ask for an up-to-date code of practice. At the same time it would be sensible to ask for an application form for membership; we would strongly recommend that you consider joining. If you are planning to form a club – for example, a book or record club – then you also should write to the Association of Mail Order Publishers and ask for details.

Another useful source of information is the *Survey of Mail Order*, produced by the Office of Fair Trading; this is obtainable from your local HMSO.

There are a great many rules and regulations contained in the various literature you will receive, but we consider it helpful to summarise the main points which, in our view, are particularly important to follow precisely. These rules apply not only to direct mail, but also to direct response advertising.

INSERTS

Recently a new form of advertising has begun to be employed by mail order advertisers in the form of inserts. These are small catalogues, brochures or leaflets which are either inserted loosely into newspapers or magazines, or sometimes stitched or stapled into those publications. In the national press they are regarded as part of the advertising content of the publication and as such advertisers must be approved by MOPS if the advertisements require the reader to send a remittance in advance of dispatch of the goods.

GOLDEN RULES OF MAIL ORDER

1. Goods must be dispatched to your customers within twenty-eight days of their order, at the latest, or within the time stipulated in your brochure – for instance, if you say delivery will be within fourteen days, then fourteen days it must be.
2. If there is going to be any delay in the dispatch of goods, the customer's order must be acknowledged and a delivery date advised. At the same time, in the acknowledgement letter, the offer must be made to send a complete refund if the customer would prefer it.
3. You must not run your business by using your customer's money. This means that you should not pay your customer's cheque into your own bank account immediately upon receipt, unless the goods are shortly to be dispatched. Quite clearly, with a cheque, you do need to allow between three and five days for clearance, and this is fully appreciated by the various trading standards authorities. However, you should not be holding on to your customer's money for any undue length of time. So far as credit cards are concerned, the legislation is even more precise. You should not debit your customer's credit card account until you are in a position to dispatch the goods, otherwise your customer may be forced to pay interest on the money, before receiving the order.
4. If the item you have sent proves unsuitable and the customer wants a replacement, alternative goods should be sent by return. If this is not possible, then the return of the goods must be acknowledged and a delivery date for replacement quoted – again, giving the customer the opportunity to seek a refund as an alternative.
5. If a refund is requested, this should be made by return and in no circumstances should a credit note be issued instead.
6. In Chapter 8 we will be dealing in detail with the layout of your brochure, but here we should mention the importance of ensuring that your full address is given on both your brochure and your order form, and that a telephone number is provided so that customers can ring if they have any problems.

If you have produced a brochure to mail to what you hope will be an increasing number of regular customers, you are clearly trying to build a stable, long-term mail order business. This being the case, all the legislation in the world is no substitute for natural courtesy and good service. If a friend wrote to you, you would reply to his letter. If a customer writes to you, whether to complain or to compliment you, you should do likewise. If, for any reason, you cannot provide the goods or service you have specified, then you must advise your customer immediately, setting out the various options that are open to him or her.

Case history

We were in the dispatch department of a clothing manufacturer one day. They had placed an advertisement in a Sunday supplement magazine, selling a dress in a choice of maroon, green or blue. Although it was the first day of dispatch, it was obvious that blue was going to be the most popular colour. On the order form, they had asked customers to quote a first and second colour choice. In many instances, customers had simply put a line through the second colour choice, but some had been co-operative and stated an alternative choice. Although the company had plenty of blue dresses in stock, in the instances where a customer had quoted a second colour choice which was not blue, they were dispatching the alternative, in order to avoid running out of blue too quickly.

We think this was a short-sighted approach. If a reader is keen enough to dispatch an order immediately, then in our view her first colour choice should be respected, while stocks last. Surely the cream of your customers must be those who react promptly to an advertisement. *It is these sort of tricks of the trade which may be good for stock control but in the long term cannot be good for the business.*

ADVERTISING STANDARDS AUTHORITY

The Advertising Standards Authority is the watchdog for all printed advertisements, whether in newspapers or magazines; nobody is free from scrutiny. As we write this book, we have one of the ASA case reports sitting in front of us, which criticises London Transport, Legal and General Assurance Society, National Westminster Bank and Sealink (UK) Ltd – to quote but a few. If big names such as these can make mistakes, it shows how careful one has to be.

We would strongly recommend that you write to the Advertising Standards Authority and ask for their *Code of Advertising Practice*. The part that is particularly relevant is Appendix F, which deals specifically with mail order.

Due to considerable advertising of their own, the Advertising Standards Authority are now well known to the public and unless you are very careful you will find that from time to time a complaint is levied against you.

Case history

This is worth repeating just to show you how extraordinary the complaints can be at times!

I (Deborah) had a call from the ASA one day. Someone had rung them to say that a shirt I had supplied was not 100 per cent cotton, as specified in the advertisement. I immediately protested, and said of course it was, but I would be very happy to send a piece of fabric to the ASA to test, if they so wished.

'No,' they replied, 'it is not the *fabric* that is being queried. The customer had made the point that the shirt is not 100 per cent cotton because the *thread* which has been used clearly is not cotton.'

Now, as anyone who does much sewing knows, nobody uses cotton thread for machining heavy-duty shirts – it is simply not strong enough. There is always some strengthening agent or a mix of fibres and, in our case, the thread we used was a poly-cotton mix.

The ASA deliberated about the problem for some time and came to the conclusion that the customer's complaint was unjustified. They stated that when an advertiser quoted the fabric content of a garment, he or she was indeed referring to the fabric, not to the thread used to sew it together. However, this demonstrates how careful you have to be!

Usually, if you are using reputable advertising agents, they should be able to assist you in ensuring that no serious blunder is made in your advertising statements. If you are advertising in a newspaper or magazine, the advertising manager will scrutinise each advertisement and he or she will advise you if he or she feels your claims may cause trouble. With your own brochure however, you must be very careful, since there is no automatic policing.

SUMMARY OF CUSTOMERS' RIGHTS

If customers are dissatisfied with your method of trading, there are many ways in which they can complain. If they have responded to an advertisement in a newspaper or magazine, they can contact the publication direct if they cannot obtain satisfaction from you. Whether or not your advertisement is covered by MOPS, they will get a very sympathetic hearing from the advertising manager of the publication in question, which may well affect your ability to advertise in the future. Alternatively, your customers may contact their local Trading Standards Department, the Consumer Protection Department, the Citizens' Advice Bureau, the Advertising Standards Authority – or even the police.

So these are the likely channels of complaint, but what actually can happen to you and your business if things start to go wrong? In the case of national newspapers, the NPA very carefully monitor the number of complaints received each week from any newspaper carrying your advertisement. Like everyone else, they know that even half a dozen complaints is probably the tip of the iceberg. For every one customer who takes the trouble to write to a newspaper, there could be literally hundreds who are dissatisfied, but so far are not doing anything about it. The NPA take complaints very seriously indeed. If there is a persistent number, over several weeks, you are likely to be suspended from newspaper advertising. Once suspended, it is far from easy to be reinstated.

In the case of the PPA, there is no central decision-making process – it is up to the individual magazine to introduce a suspension, if appropriate. However, it should be borne in mind that many magazines belong to a large group and, if you have caused a number of complaints to be sent to one magazine, you are likely to be suspended from all magazines within the group.

The industry, as a whole, is not a large one and word gets around. Chances are that if a number of complaints have been flying about, you will find it very difficult to advertise in any major publication.

If your advertisement is the subject of a complaint to the Advertising Standards Authority, and that complaint is upheld, then the ASA will ask you to withdraw or amend your advertisement accordingly. This request will be passed on to Code of Advertising Practice Committee who, in turn, will advise the media to ensure that no further advertisements in this form are accepted.

The credit card companies can take action, too. If they receive a number of complaints regarding the fact that their customers' accounts have been debited but no goods received, they will simply withdraw your right to offer credit card facilities.

With regard to the Office of Fair Trading, if a mail order trader has been the subject of persistent complaints (twenty or thirty over a year) for faulty goods, non-delivery or refunds not being given, then the OFT can take legal action under Part 3 of the Fair Trading Act. The procedure is this. The OFT will seek an assurance that there will be no further breaches of the Act. If no such assurance is given by the trader, then he or she can be taken to court – and, of course, failure to comply with the court order would be contempt of court.

The trading standard officers also have legislation at their disposal and may take local action. If they find they are unable to arrest breaches of the law then they will seek help from the OFT.

Finally, of course, there is the action of individuals themselves, who, if they can prove you have not upheld the mail order code of practice, are more than likely to win a court action against you.

Sorry, this all reads rather grimly, but *not* unfairly. Do bear in mind that your customers will only complain to 'outsiders' if they are desperate. If you provide a good service, and deal promptly with their queries and complaints, you will have no problem.

So, this chapter has outlined for you the basic legislation surrounding mail order advertising. However, we would recommend that you send for all the booklets we have recommended in this chapter and that you study them most carefully. Mistakes can prove very expensive and, in the establishment of your business, it is well worth while taking time and trouble to get things right from the very beginning.

5.   A survey of national newspapers and magazines

In this chapter, we have not attempted to list every newspaper and magazine in publication, nor have we included the regional press, since very few regional newspapers lend themselves to direct response advertising. What we are providing here is a comprehensive list of those publications, both specialist and of general interest, which we believe could prove a useful vehicle for mail order advertising. Full

addresses and telephone numbers are given in each case, together with a brief description of the publication in question, an indication as to whether it is covered by a MOPS scheme, and whether colour photography is accepted.

We have not quoted advertising rates in this chapter since these are subject to variation and, also *negotiation*. Never pay automatically the full advertising rate quoted, without first querying the possibility of a discount. When advertising revenue is slack, it is quite possible to obtain very substantial discounts – this particularly applies at certain times of the year, such as Christmas. The Sunday supplements, for example, have been known to discount up to 60 per cent in some circumstances. If you are placing a series of advertisements in a single publication, then, most certainly, you should expect a discount. Similarly, if you are placing a last-minute advertisement, you can very often do a quite amazing deal if space is still available. Indeed, once you are an established name in mail order, you will find that the publications in which you regularly advertise will telephone you from time to time when they have unexpected space to fill. In these circumstances there is often some very cheap advertising to be had. For this reason, you should not be working too far ahead in terms of booking space. Never commit yourself to a year's advertising, or even six months. Retain as much flexibility in your booking as you can so that you can take advantage of cheap deals without overspending your budget.

When looking at newspapers and magazines, you should not be restricting your thinking purely to taking advertising space. One of the most popular methods of advertising these days is the *insert*. Inserts cost between £20 and £40 per thousand. Of course, in addition, there is the cost of printing the insert leaflet, but, by and large, the whole exercise is still considerably cheaper than taking advertising space. It also gives you the opportunity to sell many more products – in fact the absolute minimum number of products you should sell from an insert is six. Inserts have a long shelf life, they hang around in the home – and they often survive far longer than their host publication, particularly when compared with newspapers. Not all magazines and newspapers are prepared to take inserts, but we would recommend that you seriously consider this form of advertising. An important point to note is that inserts are covered by MOPS in all publications which subscribe to the scheme for their general direct response advertising.

We hope this information will be helpful to you, in trying to decide where to place your advertising.

Publications

Amateur Gardening
Westover House
West Quay Road
Poole
Dorset BH15 1JG
(0202) 671191
MOPS. Colour.
Covers all aspects of gardening.
Price: 40p. Weekly.

Amateur Photographer
Surrey House
Throwley Way
Sutton
Surrey SM1 4QQ
01–643 8040

MOPS. Colour.
Instructional magazine giving
details of latest equipment and
techniques.
Price: 60p. Weekly.

Angler's Mail
IPC Magazines Ltd
King's Reach Tower
Stamford Street
London SE1 9LS
01–261 5829
MOPS. Colour.
Angling news magazine – sea,
coarse and game fishing.
Price: 40p. Weekly.

Angling Times
EMAP
Bretton Court
Bretton
Peterborough PE3 8DZ
(0733) 266222
MOPS. Colour.
Largest circulation angling
publication – newspaper format.
Price: 38p. Weekly.

Annabel
D. C. Thomson and Co. Ltd
80 Kingsway East
Dundee DD4 8SL
and
185 Fleet Street
London EC4A 2HS
(0382) 44276
MOPS. Colour.
Magazine for modern women –
married and single.
Price: 45p. Monthly.

Antique Collector
National Magazine House
72 Broadwick Street
London W1V 2BP
01–439 7144
MOPS. Colour.
Aimed at private collectors and
the trade.
Price: £1.50. Monthly.

Architects' Journal
9 Queen Anne's Gate
London SW1H 9BY
01–222 4333
MOPS. Colour.
The only technical publication
for architects.
Price: 90p. Weekly.

Art and Artists
43b Gloucester Road
Croydon CR0 2DH
01–240 2032

MOPS. Colour.
Deals with all aspects of the
visual arts – as an amateur or as
a professional.
Price: £1.25. Monthly.

Autocar
Haymarket Publishing Ltd
38/42 Hampton Road
Teddington
Middlesex TW11 0JE
01–977 8787
MOPS. Colour.
Motoring magazine on all
aspects of the industry.
Price: 60p. Weekly.

Boards
196 Eastern Esplanade
Southend-on-Sea
Essex SS1 3AB
(0702) 582245
Colour.
Magazine for windsurfers and
board sailors.
Price: 95p. Monthly in summer,
bi-monthly in winter.

Bookseller, The
J. Whitaker and Sons Ltd
12 Dyott Street
London WC1A 1DF
01–836 8911
Colour.
Publishers' and booksellers'
trade magazine.
Price: 65p. Weekly.

British Medical Journal
British Medical Association
House
Tavistock Square
London WC1H 9JR
01–387 4499
MOPS. Colour.
All aspects of the medical
world.
Price: £2.25. Weekly.

British Printer
76 Oxford Street
LondonW1N 2FD
01–434 2233
Colour.
Technical magazine on all
aspects of printing and graphics
Price: £20 p.a. Monthly

Cage and Aviary Birds
Surrey House
1 Throwley Way
Sutton
Surrey SM1 4QQ
01–643 8040
MOPS. Colour.
Aviculture and ornithology
generally.
Price: 40p. Weekly.

*Camera and Creative
Photography*
EMAP
Bushfield House
Orton Centre
Peterborough PE2 OUW
(0733) 237111
MOPS. Colour.
For amateur and professional
photographers.
Price: £1.35. Monthly.

Campaign
22 Lancaster Gate
London W2 3LY
01–402 4200 and 5266
Colour.
Magazine of the media –
advertising, marketing,
publishing, TV, printing, PR.
Price: 60p. Weekly.

Camping and Trailer
Link House
Dingwall Avenue
Croydon CR9 2TA
01–686 2599
MOPS. Colour.

Camping and touring – reports
and advice.
Price: 80p. Monthly.

Car
64 West Smithfield
London EC1A 9EE
01–606 7836
Colour
All aspects of cars and car driving.
Price: £1. Monthly.

Car Mechanics
Audit House
Field End Road
Eastcote
Ruislip
Middlesex HA4 9LT
01–868 4499
Line and half tone.
Car maintenance and repair.
Price: 80p. Monthly.

Caravan
Link House
Dingwall Avenue
Croydon CR9 2TA.
01–686 2599
MOPS. Colour.
All aspects of touring and
caravanning.
Price: 80p. Monthly.

Catering and Hotel Keeper
Quadrant House
The Quadrant
Sutton
Surrey SM2 5AS
01–661 3500
MOPS. Colour.
General catering – food service,
hotels.
Price: £1. Monthly.

Choice Magazine
Bedford Chambers
Covent Garden
London WC2E 8HA
01–836 8772

Colour.
Magazine of fiction and features
aimed at retired people.
Price: 80p. Monthly.

Classical Music
52a Floral Street
London WC2E 9DA
01–836 2383
Colour.
All aspects of classical music –
record reviews, notice of
concerts.
Price: 50p. Fortnightly.

Climber and Rambler
Harmony Hall
Milnthorpe
Cumbria
041 221 7000
Colour.
Official journal of the British
Mountaineering Council. Covers
mountaineering and hill walking.
Price: 90p. Monthly.

Commercial Motor
IPC Transport Press Ltd
Quadrant House
The Quadrant
Sutton
Surrey SM2 5AS
01–661 3500
MOPS. Colour.
Technical magazine on all
aspects of road transport.
Price: 50p. Weekly.

Company
National Magazine House
72 Broadwick Street
London W1V 2BP
01–439 7144
MOPS. Colour.
Aimed at modern women –
probably with a career.
Price: 75p. Monthly.

Cosmetic World News
130 Wigmore Street
London W1H OAT
01–486 6757–8
Colour.
Magazine for the cosmetic,
perfumery and general toiletries
industry.
Price: £39 p. a. Monthly.

Cosmopolitan
National Magazine House
72 Broadwick Street
London, W1V 2BP
01–439 7144
MOPS. Colour.
Young woman's magazine –
features and fiction.
Price: 75p. Monthly.

Country Life
IPC Magazines
King's Reach Tower
Stamford Street
London SE1 9LS
01–261 7058
MOPS. Colour.
Specialises in articles on English
country life, arts and gardening.
Big property section.
Price: 90p. Weekly.

Countryman, The
Sheep Street
Burford
Oxford OX8 4LH
(099 382) 2000
Black and white photographs
and line drawings.
All aspects of rural life, except
field sports.
Price: £1. Quarterly.

Creative Camera
Coo Press Ltd
19 Doughty Street
London WC1N 2PT
01–405 7562

Black and white photographs,
line drawings. Dealing with the
art of photography, rather than
equipment. Arts Council
Support.
Price: £1.50. Monthly.

Cricketer International, The
29 Cavendish Road
Redhill
Surrey RH1 4AH
(0737) 68433
MOPS. Colour.
All aspects of the game.
Price: 90p. Monthly.

Cycling
Surrey House
1 Throwley Way
Sutton
Surrey SM1 4QQ
01–643 8040
MOPS. Colour.
All aspects of cycling
interest.
Price: 50p. Weekly.

Daily Express
121 Fleet Street
London EC4P 4JT
01–353 8000
Great Ancoats Street
Manchester M60 4HB
061–236 2112
MOPS. Colour.
National newspaper.
Price: 20p. Daily.

Daily Mail
Northcliffe House
London EC4Y 0JA
01–353 6000
MOPS. Colour.
National newspaper now
incorporating *News Chronicle*
and *Daily Sketch*.
Price: 20p. Daily.

Daily Mirror
Holborn Circus
London EC1P 1DQ
01–353 0246
MOPS. Colour.
National newspaper.
Price: 18p. Daily.

Daily Star
Great Ancoats Street
Manchester M60 4HB
061–236 9575
MOPS. Colour.
National newspaper.
Price: 18p. Daily.

Daily Telegraph, The
135 Fleet Street
London EC4P 4BL
01–353 4242
MOPS. Colour.
National newspaper.
Price: 25p. Daily.

Darts World
World Magazines Ltd
2 Park Lane
Croydon
Surrey CR9 1HA
01–681 2837
Colour.
All aspects of the sport.
Price: 70p. Monthly.

DIY Today
Sovereign House
Brentwood
Essex CM14 4SE
(0277) 219876
Colour.
All DIY subjects covered.
Price: 70p. Monthly.

Do It Yourself
Link House
Dingwall Avenue
Croydon CR9 2TA
01–686 2599

Colour.
Covers DIY in house and
garden.
Price: 70p. Monthly.

Drapers Record
Knightway House
20 Soho Square
London W1V 6DT
01–734 1255
Colour.
Magazine for the fashion and
textile retail and wholesale
trade.
Price: 65p. Weekly.

Embroidery
The Embroiderers' Guild
PO Box 42B
East Molesey
Surrey KT8 9BB
01–943 1229
Colour.
General articles on the art of
embroidery.
Price: £1.10. Quarterly.

Exchange and Mart
Link House
25 West Street
Poole
Dorset BH15 1LL
(0202) 671171
Line drawings.
The classified advertising
magazine.
Price: 35p. Weekly.

Family Circle
Elm House
Elm Street
London WC1X 0BP
01–278 2345
MOPS. Colour.
Practical women's magazine.
Price: 42p. Monthly.

Farmers Weekly

Agriculture and Construction
Press
Surrey House
1 Throwley Way
Sutton
Surrey SM1 4QQ
01–643 8040
MOPS. Black and white
illustrations.
All aspects of agriculture.
Price: 45p. Weekly.

Field, The
Carmelite House
Carmelite Street
London EC4Y 0JA
01–353 6000
MOPS. Colour.
Country pursuits in the British
countryside.
Price: 60p. Weekly.

Films and Filming
43b Gloucester Road
Croydon CR0 2DH
01–689 4104
Line, half-tone.
Magazine on serious cinema.
Price: 90p. Monthly.

Financial Times
Bracken House
10 Cannon Street
London EC4P 4BY
01–248 8000
MOPS. Colour.
National newspaper.
Price: 40p. Daily.

Financial Weekly
Maxwell House
74 Worship Street
London EC2A 2EN
01–377 4600.
MOPS. Line and half-tone.
General aspects of financial and
commercial concern.
Price: 75p. Weekly.

*Freelance Writing and
Photography*
5–9 Bexley Square
Salford
Manchester M3 6DB
061–832 5079
Line and half-tone.
Magazine aimed at the freelance
writer and photographer.
Price: £4.50 p.a. Quarterly.

Fruit Trades Journal
430 Market Towers
New Covent Garden
Nine Elms Lane
London SW8 5NN
01–720 8822.
Line and half-tone.
All aspects of importing and
distribution.
Price: 60p. Weekly.

Garden News
Bushfield House
Orton Centre
Peterborough PE2 0UW
(0733) 237111
MOPS. Colour.
General gardening features.
Price: 32p. Weekly.

Golf Monthly
1 Park Circus
Glasgow G3 6AS
041–332 2828
Colour.
General features on golfing.
Price: 95p. Monthly.

Golf World
Millstream House
41 Maltby Street
London SE1 3PA
01–237 3011
Colour.
All aspects of the game.
Price: £1. Monthly.

Good Housekeeping
National Magazine House
72 Broadwick Street
London W1V 2BP
01–439 7144
MOPS. Colour.
Magazine for the intelligent,
domestic woman.
Price: 70p. Monthly.

Great Outdoors, The
Ravenseft House
302 St Vincent Street
Glasgow G2 5NL
041–221 7000
Colour.
General aspects of walking and
climbing.
Price: 80p. Monthly.

Grower, The
50 Doughty Street
London WC1N 2LP
01–405 0364
MOPS. Colour.
Commercial horticulture.
Price: 50p. Weekly.

Guardian, The
119 Farringdon Road
London EC1
01–278 2332 and
164 Deansgate
Manchester M60 2RR
061–832 7200
MOPS. Colour.
National newspaper.
Price: 25p. Daily.

Harper's and Queen
National Magazine House
72 Broadwick Street
London W1V 2BP
01–439 7144
MOPS. Colour.
Features and fashion for
women.
Price: £1.50. Monthly.

Health and Efficiency
International
23–4 Smithfield Street
London EC1
01–236 4511
Colour.
General aspects of naturalist
and health matters.
Price: 90p. Monthly.

Hi-fi News and Record Review
Link House
Dingwall Avenue
Croydon CR9 2TA
01–686 2599
Colour.
All aspects of sound recording.
Price: £1. Monthly.

Home and Family
The Mothers' Union
The Mary Sumner House
24 Tufton Street
London SW1P 3RB
01–248 6085
Line and half-tone.
Aspects of Christian family
life.
Price: 23p. Quarterly.

Homes and Gardens
IPC Magazines
King's Reach Tower
Stamford Street
London SE1 9LS
01–261 6099
MOPS. Colour.
General aspects of the home –
for men and women.
Price: 75p. Monthly.

Honey
IPC Magazines
King's Reach Tower
Stamford Street
London SE1 9LS
01–261 5240

MOPS. Colour.
Aimed at women eighteen to
twenty-eight years old.
Price: 50p. Monthly.

Horse and Hound
IPC Magazines
King's Reach Tower
Stamford Street
London SE1 9LS
01–261 6315
MOPS. Line and half-tone.
All aspects of horses and
hunting.
Price: 60p. Weekly.

Horse and Pony
EMAP Nationals
Bretton Court
Bretton
Peterborough PE3 8DZ
(0733) 268811
MOPS. Colour.
All matters related to
equestrian interests.
Price: 55p. Fortnightly.

Horse and Rider
104 Ash Road
Sutton
Surrey SM3 9LD
01–641 4911
Colour.
Equestrian activities at home
and abroad.
Price: 70p. Monthly.

Hospitality
Low Level
82 Hungerford Road
London N7X 8LS
01–240 2032
Colour.
Official magazine of the Hotel
Catering and Institutional
Management Association.
Price: £1.75. Monthly.

House and Garden
Vogue House
Hanover Square
London W1R 0AD
01–499 9080
MOPS. Colour.
All subjects related to interior
decorating, furnishing and
gardening.
Price: £1.20. Monthly.

Ideal Home
King's Reach Tower
Stamford Street
London SE1 9LS
01–261 6474
MOPS. Colour.
All aspects related to the home.
Price: 80p. Monthly.

Illustrated London News
Elm House
10–16 Elm Street
London WC1X 0BP
01–278 2345
MOPS. Colour.
A general news magazine.
Price: £1.20. Monthly.

In Britain
British Tourist Authority
239 Old Marylebone Road
London NW1 5QT
01–262 0141
MOPS. Colour.
Features magazine on all
aspects of Britain.
Price: 85p. Monthly.

Investors Chronicle
Greystoke Place
Fetter Lane
London EC4A 1ND
01–405 6969
MOPS. Colour.
Leading journal for investment
and general business matters.
Price: 95p. Weekly.

Lady, The
39–40 Bedford Street
Strand
London WC2E 9ER
01–836 8705
MOPS. Colour.
Human interest magazine –
covers the countryside, travel
and domestic matters.
Price: 38p. Weekly.

Living
Elm House
Elm Street
London WC1X 0BP
01–278 2345
MOPS. Colour.
General interest women's
magazine.
Price: 42p. Monthly.

Look Now
27 Newman Stret
London W1P 3PE
01–637 9671
Line drawings.
Fashion and general articles for
women aged seventeen to
twenty-three.
Price: 60p. Monthly.

Loving
IPC Magazines Ltd
King's Reach Tower
Stamford Street
London SE1 9LS
01–261 6510
MOPS. Colour.
First-person real-life stories,
aimed at girls and women in
their teens and early twenties.
Price: 26p. Weekly.

Mail on Sunday
Northcliffe House
London EC4Y 0JA
01–353 6000

MOPS. Colour.
Sunday supplement magazine.
Price: 40p. Weekly.

Melody Maker
IPC Magazines Limited
Berkshire House
168–173 High Holborn
London WC1V 7AU
01–379 3581
MOPS. Half-tone and line
drawings.
Rock and pop music.

Model Boats
Model and Allied
Publications
PO Box 35
Hemel Hempstead
Herts HPZ 4SS
(0442) 41221
Line, half-tone.
All aspects of model boats and
boating.
Price: 95p. Monthly.

Model Engineer
Model and Allied
Publications
PO Box 35,
Hemel Hempstead ⁓
Herts HPZ 4SS
(0442) 41221
Half-tone and line drawings.
All aspects of model
construction.
Price: 70p. Monthly.

Mother
Commonwealth House
1–19 New Oxford Street
London WC1A 1NG
01–404 0700
MOPS. Colour.
All aspects of bringing up
young children.
Price: 65p. Monthly.

Motor
Surrey House
1 Throwley Way
Sutton
Surrey SM1 4QQ
01–643 8040
Colour.
Articles on topical motoring
matters.
Price: 55p. Weekly.

Motor Boat and Yachting
Business Press International
Ltd
Quadrant House
Sutton
Surrey SM2 5AS
01–661 3098
Colour.
General aspects of motor
boating.
Price: £1.10. Monthly.

*Motorcaravan and Motorhome
Monthly*
20 Barons Walk
Lewes
Sussex BN7 1EX
(07916) 6668
Colour.
All aspects of motor-caravan
travel.
Price: 70p. Monthly.

My Weekly
D. C. Thomson and Co.
Ltd
80 Kingsway East
Dundee DD4 8SL
and
185 Fleet Street
London EC4A 2HS
0382 44276
MOPS. Colour.
General family magazine –
features and fiction.
Price: 18p. Weekly.

New Musical Express
3rd Floor
5–7 Carnaby Street
London W1V 1PG
01–439 8761
Colour.
All aspects of the rock music
scene.
Price: 40p. Weekly.

News of the World
30 Bouverie Street
London EC4Y 8EX
01–353 3030
MOPS. Colour.
National Sunday newspaper.
Price: 28p. Weekly.

19
King's Reach Tower
Stamford Street
London SE1 9LS
01–261 6360
MOPS. Colour.
Fashion magazine for young
women.
Price: 65p. Monthly.

Nursing Times
Macmillan Journals Ltd
4 Little Essex Street
London WC2R 3LF
01–836 1776
MOPS. Colour.
General aspects of nursing.
Price: 35p. Weekly.

Observer
8 St Andrew's Hill
London EC4V 5JA
01–236 0202
MOPS. Colour.
National Sunday newspaper.
Price: 50p. Weekly.

Observer Colour Magazine
8 St Andrew's Hill
London EC4V 5JA
01–236 0202

MOPS. Colour.
Supplement to the newspaper.
Price: free with newspaper.

Options
27 Newman Street
London W1P 3PE
01–637 9671
MOPS. Colour.
General interest women's
magazine.
Price: 70p. Monthly.

Over 21
Wellington House
6–9 Upper St Martin's Lane
London WC2H 9EX
01–836 0142
MOPS. Colour.
General features aimed at mod-
ern women.
Price: 70p. Monthly.

Parents
116 Newgate Street
London EC1A 7AE
01–726 6999
MOPS. Colour.
All aspects of child upbringing
and family life.
Price: 70p. Monthly.

People's Friend
D. C. Thomson and Co. Ltd
80 Kingsway East
Dundee DD4 8SL
and
185 Fleet Street
London EC4A 2HS
0382 44276
MOPS. Colour.
Women's magazine with high
fiction content.
Price: 18p. Weekly.

Photography
Model and Allied Publications
PO Box 35

Hemel Hempstead
Herts HP2 4SS
(0442) 41221
Colour.
Aimed at serious amateur and
professional photographers.
Price: 85p. Monthly.

Pony
104 Ash Road
Sutton
Surrey SM3 9LD
01–641 4911
Colour.
Aimed at young horse riders
aged ten to eighteen.
Price: 70p. Monthly.

Popular Caravan
Sovereign House
Brentwood
Essex CM14 4SE
(0277) 219 876
Colour.
All aspects of caravanning.
Price: 80p. Monthly.

Popular Crafts
(incorporating *Gem Craft*)
PO Box 35
Hemel Hempstead
Herts HP2 4SS
(0442) 41221
Transparencies and half-tone.
Useful guidance on crafts in
general.
Price: 95p. Monthly.

Popular Gardening
King's Reach Tower
Stamford Street
London SE1 9LS
01–261 5787
MOPS. Colour.
Magazine for amateur and
professional gardeners.
Price: 12p. Weekly.

Poultry World
Surrey House
1 Throwley Way
Sutton
Surrey SM1 4QQ
01–643 8040
MOPS. Black and white
photographs and line drawings.
All aspects of commercial
poultry breeding and
marketing.
Price: 45p. Weekly.

Power Farming
Agricultural and Construction
Press Ltd
Surrey House
1 Throwley Way
Sutton
Surrey SM1 4QQ
01–643 8040
MOPS. Colour.
All aspects of farm machinery.
Price: 85p. Monthly.

Practical Boat Owner
Westover House
West Quay Road
Poole
Dorset BH15 1JG
(0202) 671191
Black and white photographs
and line drawings.
Practical advice for boating
enthusiasts.
Price: £1. Monthly.

Practical Camper
Haymarket Publishing Ltd
38–42 Hampton Road
Teddington
Middlesex TW11 0JE
01–977 8787
MOPS. Line drawings.
General matters of interest
regarding camping and touring.
Price: 75p. Monthly.

Practical Computing
Quadrant House
The Quadrant
Sutton
Surrey SM2 5AS
01–661 3609
Black and white photographs
and line drawings.
Magazine for people generally
interested in computers.
Price: 85p. Monthly.

Practical Fishkeeping
EMAP National Publications
Bretton Court
Bretton
Peterborough PE3 8DZ
(0733) 264666
MOPS. Colour.
General aspects of fishkeeping.
Price: 85p. Monthly.

Practical Gardening
Bushfield House
Orton Centre
Peterborough PE2 0UW
(0733) 237111
MOPS. Colour.
All gardening subjects of general
interest.
Price: 75p. Monthly.

Practical Householder
Westover House
West Quay Road
Poole
Dorset BH15 1JG
(0202) 671191
MOPS. Colour.
All aspects of home
improvement.
Price: 70p. Monthly.

Practical Photography
EMAP
Bushfield House
Orton Centre
Peterborough PE2 0UW
(0733) 237111

MOPS. Colour.
Practical photography.
Price: 90p. Monthly.

Practical Wireless
IPC Magazines Ltd
Westover House
West Quay Road
Poole
Dorset BH15 1JG
(0202) 671191
MOPS. Colour.
Magazine for amateur radio
enthusiasts.
Price: 48p. Monthly.

Practical Woodworking
King's Reach Tower
Stamford Street
London SE1 9LS
01–261 6602
MOPS. Black and white
photographs and line drawings.
General aspects of
woodworking.
Price: 95p. Monthly.

Printing World
Benn Publications Ltd
Benn House
Sovereign Way
Tonbridge
Kent TN9 1RW
(0732) 364422
MOPS. Colour.
Technical publication for
printing industry.
Price: 70p. Weekly.

Private Eye
6 Carlisle Street
London W1V 5RG
01–437 4017
Black and white photographs
and line drawings.
Satirical magazine.
Price: 40p. Fortnightly.

Publishing News
43 Museum Street
London WC1A 1LY
01–404 0304
Half-tones.
Magazine for publishers and
the book trade generally.
Price: 60p. Fortnightly.

Punch
23–27 Tudor Street
London EC4Y 0HR
01–583 9199
MOPS. Line drawings and
half-tones.
Humorous magazine, reporting
contemporary events.
Price: 45p. Weekly.

Radio Times
BBC Publications
35 Marylebone High Street
London W1M 4AA
01–580 5577
Journal of the BBC.
Price: 28p. Weekly.

Railway Magazine
Quadrant House
The Quadrant
Sutton
Surrey SM2 5AS
01 -661 3694
MOPS. Colour.
All railway subjects
covered.
Price: 75p. Monthly.

Reader's Digest
The Reader's Digest
Association Ltd
25 Berkeley Square
London W1X 6AB
01–629 8144
MOPS. Colour.
General features and
stories.
Price: £1. Monthly.

Riding
IPC Magazines
King's Reach Tower
Stamford Street
London SE1 9LS
01–261 5487
MOPS. Colour.
General information on the
caring of horses.
Price: 80p. Monthly.

Sea Angler
EMAP National Publications Ltd
Bretton Court
Bretton
Peterborough PE3 8DZ
(0733) 264666
MOPS. Colour.
All aspects of sea fishing.
Price: 75p. Monthly.

Secrets
D. C. Thomson and Co. Ltd
Courier Place
Dundee DD1 9QJ
0382 23131
and
185 Fleet Street
London EC4A 2HS
01–242 4971
MOPS. Colour.
Fiction magazine for women of
all ages.
Price: 16p. Weekly.

She
National Magazine House
72 Broadwick Street
London W1V 2BP
01–439 7144
MOPS. Colour.
Magazine for modern women.
Price: 65p. Monthly.

Ship and Boat International
16 Lower Marsh
London SE1 7RJ
01–330 4311

MOPS. Colour.
Technical magazine concerned
with design of small ships.
Price: £33 p.a. 10 issues p.a.

*Shooting Times and Country
Magazine*
Burlington Publishing Co. Ltd
10 Sheet Street
Windsor
Berkshire SL4 1BG
(07535) 56061
MOPS. Colour.
Covers all field sports and matters
concerning the countryside.
Price: 60p. Weekly.

Short Wave Magazine, The
34 High Street
Welwyn
Herts Al6 9EQ
(043871) 5206–7
Line drawings, half-tones.
Technical magazine for amateur
radio enthusiasts.
Price: 65p. Monthly.

Ski Magazine
Ocean Publications Ltd
34 Buckingham Palace Road
London SW1W 0RE
01–828 4551
Colour.
All aspects of skiing
Price: £1. Bi-monthly.

Sporting Life
Mirror Group Newspapers Ltd
9 New Fetter Lane
London EC4A 1AR
01–353 0246.
MOPS. Colour.
National newspaper.
Price: 40p. Daily.

Stage and Television Today
Stage House
47 Bermondsey Street
London SE1 3XT

01–403 1818
Colour.
Specialist magazine for
professionals.
Price: 25p. Weekly.

Stamp Lover
National Philatelic Society
London International Stamp
Centre
27 King Street
London WC2E 8JD
01–836 6294 and 01–240 7349
Black and white photographs
and line drawings.
All aspects of stamps and their
history.
Price: 60p. Quarterly.

Stamp Magazine
Link House
Dingwall Avenue
Croydon CR9 2TA
01–686 2599
Colour.
General magazine on the
subject.
Price: 85p. Monthly.

Stamp Monthly
Drury Lane
Russell Street
London WC2B 5HD
01–836 8444
Black and white photographs.
General articles on the
subject.
Price: 85p. Monthly.

Stamps and Foreign Stamps
EMAP National Publications
Bushfield House
Orton Centre
Peterborough PE2 0UW
MOPS. Colour.
All aspects on the subject
covered.
Price: 80p. Monthly.

Standard, The
PO Box 136
118–21 Fleet Street
London EC4P 4JT
01–353 8000
MOPS. Colour.
Evening newspaper – London
and the Home Counties.
Price: 18p. Daily.

Store Planning and Design
AGB Westbourne Ltd
Audit House
Field End Road
Eastcote
Ruislip
Middlesex HA4 9XE
01–868 4499
Colour.
Technical publication on store
design.
Price: £2. Monthly.

Studio Sound
Link House
Dingwall Avenue
Croydon CR9 2TA
01–686 2599
Colour.
All aspects of sound recording.
Price: £1. Monthly.

Sun, The
News Group Newspapers Ltd
30 Bouverie Street
London EC4Y 8DE
01–353 3030
MOPS. Colour.
National newspaper.
Price: 18p. Daily.

Sunday Express
Fleet Street
London EC4P 4JT
01–353 8000
MOPS. Colour.
Sunday national newspaper.
Price: 35p. Weekly.

Sunday Express Magazine
11 New Fetter Lane
London EC4P 4EE
01–353 8000
MOPS. Colour.
Sunday colour supplement
magazine.
Free with the newspaper. Weekly.

Sunday Magazine
18 Ogle Street
London W1P 7LG
01–635 5010
MOPS. Colour.
Sunday colour supplement
magazine.
Free with the *News of the World*.
Weekly.

Sunday Mirror
33 Holborn
London EC1P 1DQ
01–353 0246
MOPS. Colour.
National Sunday newspaper.
Price: 28p. Weekly.

Sunday People
Orbit House
9 New Fetter Lane
London EC4A 1AR
01–353 0246
MOPS. Colour.
National Sunday newspaper.
Price: 28p. Weekly.

Sunday Sun, The
Thomson House
Groat Market
Newcastle NE1 1ED
0632 327500
MOPS. Colour.
Sunday newspaper.
Price: 24p. Weekly.

Sunday Telegraph
135 Fleet Street
London EC4P 4BL
01–353 4242

MOPS. Colour.
National Sunday magazine.
Price: 40p. Weekly.

Sunday Times
200 Gray's Inn Road
London WC1X 8EZ
01–837 1234
MOPS. Colour.
National Sunday newspaper.
Price: 50p. Weekly.

Sunday Times Magazine
200 Gray's Inn Road
London WC1X 8EZ
01–837 1234
MOPS. Colour.
Sunday colour supplement
magazine.
Free with newspaper weekly.

Tatler, The
Vogue House
Hanover Square
London W1R 0AD
01–499 9080
MOPS. Colour.
Society magazine.
Price: £1.20. 10 issues p.a.

Telegraph Sunday Magazine
135 Fleet Street
London EC4P 4BL
01–353 4242
MOPS. Colour.
Sunday colour supplement
magazine.
Free with newspaper weekly.

Television
IPC Magazines Ltd
King's Reach Tower
Stamford Street
London SE1 9LS
01–261 5752
MOPS. Colour.
Technical magazine on the
industry generally.
Price: £1. Monthly.

Tennis
34 Buckingham Palace Road,
London SW1W 0RE
01–828 4551
Colour.
All aspects of the game.
Price: 80p. 8 issues p.a.

Times, The
200 Gray's Inn Road
London WC1X 8EZ
01–837 1234
MOPS. Colour
National newspaper.
Price: 25p. Daily.

Today
News (UK) Ltd
70 Vauxhall Bridge Road
London SW1V 2RP
01–630 1333
MOPS. Colour
National Sunday and daily
newspaper.
Price 18p weekday. 30p
Sunday.

Trout and Salmon
EMAP
Bretton Court
Bretton Centre
Peterborough PE3 8DZ
(0733) 264666
MOPS. Colour.
All aspects of trout and salmon
fishing.
Price: 85p. Monthly.

True Romances
Argus Press
12–18 Paul Street
London EC2A 4JS
01–247 8233
MOPS. Colour.
First-person true-love
stories.
Price: 65p. Monthly.

True Story
Argus Press
12–18 Paul Street
London EC2A 4JS
01–247 8233
MOPS. Colour.
First-person true-love stories.
Price: 65p. Monthly.

TV Times Magazine
247 Tottenham Court Road
London W1P 0AU
01–636 3666
MOPS. Colour.
Guide to independent
broadcasting stations' pro-
grammes.
Price: 28p. Weekly.

Vegetarian, The
Parkdale
Dunham Road
Altrincham
Cheshire WA14 4QG
061–928 0793
Colour.
Nutrition and animal welfare.
Price: 40p. Bi-monthly.

Vogue
Vogue House
Hanover Square
London W1R 0AD
01–499 9080
MOPS. Colour.
Fashion and beauty for
sophisticated women.
Price: £1.60. Monthly.

Weekend
Northcliffe House
London EC4Y 0JA
01–353 6000
MOPS. Colour.
Family magazine containing
general features.
Price: 24p. Weekly.

Woman
King's Reach Tower
Stamford Street
London SE1 9LS
01–261 5413
MOPS. Colour.
Widely read by all types of
women.
Price: 26p. Weekly.

Woman and Home
King's Reach Tower
Stamford Street
London SE1 9LS
01–261 5423
MOPS. Colour.
For women with a career
and/or a family.
Price: 65p. Monthly.

Woman's Journal
King's Reach Tower
Stamford Street
London SE1 9LS
01–261 6622
MOPS. Colour.
Aimed at intelligent women.
Price: 75p. Monthly.

Woman's Own
King's Reach Tower
Stamford Street
London SE1 9LS
01–261 5474
MOPS. Colour.
For modern women of all
ages.
Price: 26p. Weekly.

Woman's Realm
King's Reach Tower
Stamford Street
London SE1 9LS
01–261 6244
MOPS. Colour.
Primarily aimed at women with
families.
Price: 24p. Weekly.

Woman's Story Magazine
Argus Press
12–18 Paul Street
London EC2A 4JS
01–247 8233
MOPS. Colour.
Short story magazine.
Price: 65p. Monthly.

Woman's Weekly
King's Reach Tower
Stamford Street
London SE1 9LS
01–261 6131
MOPS. Colour.
Family magazine.
Price: 25p. Weekly.

Woman's World
27 Newman Street
London W1P 3PE
01–637 9671
MOPS. Colour.
Aimed at women today.
Price: 65p. Monthly.

World Fishing
Nortide Ltd
Ashford House
The Tufton Centre
Ashford
Kent TN23 1YB
(0233) 39961–4

Colour.
Technical magazine on all
aspects of catching and
marketing fish.
Price: £27 p.a. Monthly.

Yachting Monthly
Room 2209
King's Reach Tower
Stamford Street
London SE1 9LS
01–261 6040
MOPS. Colour.
All aspects of sailing, including
design, construction and
equipment.
Price £1.10. Monthly.

Yachting World
Business Press International Ltd
Quadrant House
The Quadrant
Sutton
Surrey SM2 5AS
01–661 3864
MOPS. Colour.
All aspects of boats and sailing.
Price: £1. Monthly.

6.   Advertising agents

In our other business guidebooks, on a number of occasions we have indicated our lack of faith in the value of advertising agents to the average small business. However, this is *not* our view where mail order businesses are concerned.

If you are intending to launch a direct response advertising campaign, even on a modest level, we strongly recommend the use of an advertising agent. Frankly, you are moving into an industry where you can do with all the help you can get. The one proviso we would add to this piece of advice is that the agency you choose *must have direct response mail order experience*. There is a great deal of information you need to know: which magazines are likely to prove best for a certain type of product; which times of the year you should, and should not, advertise; where the best discount deals are to be had; etc. etc. You must be able to draw on someone who has this sort of information and experience readily to hand.

If you have no previous experience of advertising agents and do not know of anyone who can recommend an agency, then we would suggest you invest in The *Creative Handbook*. It can be obtained from the address given at the end of this book. In the *Creative Handbook* you will find not only a list of advertising agencies, but also public relations companies, photographers and model agencies. It is a very useful book to have around.

In your search for the right agency, do not allow yourself to become carried away by all the patter which normally surrounds these people. The first quality a good mail order agency must have is direct response experience. What are the others?

1. They do not need to be a large agency – in fact, quite the contrary. We would recommend you look first at smaller agencies, where your account is going to be important to them.
2. You need to instinctively like and trust your agency. Remember, on their advice you are going to be spending certainly hundreds if not many thousands of pounds.
3. We would recommend that you go for a London-based agency, or, if not, a provincial agency with a London office. The reason for this is that your agency will be negotiating with the media on your behalf. If they are London-based, they will probably know personally many of the advertising managers; they are therefore far more likely to negotiate a better deal.
4. Do not commit yourself to an advertising agency that insists on providing the full advertising package. Do not be bullied into allowing them to handle your catalogue design and printing, nor your public relations. Initially, you should be looking at a relationship which is restricted to the placing of advertising space. If they are not prepared to do this, then forget them.
5. Suspect an agency that is full of ideas for spending your money. Ones that preach caution are likely to be the most useful.

Now let us look at the mechanics of the relationship with your advertising agent. In order for an advertising agency to represent you in direct response advertising, they have to be accepted by the various MOPS schemes; this will mean their paying a fee to the various bodies such as the NPA and PPA. These organisations, in turn, keep a register of advertising agencies and are just as anxious to see that agencies are following the laid-down codes of practice as the advertisers themselves. The advertising agent is responsible for booking space and for paying the advertising costs. In turn, they will bill you.

When an advertising agent places an advertisement with a publication, he or she is automatically given a 15 per cent discount; it is this 15 per cent which represents his or her fee, that is, payment for arranging your advertising. If you place an advertisement direct, in theory you do not receive this discount. However, if you are a large enough organisation, regularly booking space, you can probably do as good a deal as any agency.

Because of the nature of the booking relationship, clearly your advertising agent is going to want some form of reassurance that you are going to be able to pay your advertising fees. Normally, agencies bill their clients once a month, but it may be that early on in your relationship they will ask for immediate settlement, or even payment in advance. Agencies have to be very strict when it comes to settlement of advertising fees – not only from their own cash-flow point of view, but also because they are required, under the terms of the MOP scheme, to advise all concerned if the advertiser is unable to settle his or her fees. In these circumstances, no future advertising would be accepted until the advertiser had regularised his or her financial position, the thinking being that if the advertiser cannot pay the agency, he or she may not be able to service the customers. Failure on the part of the agency to advise publications of an advertiser's financial troubles could land the agency in serious trouble: he or she might loose the right to book space.

The Institute of Practitioners in Advertising have a code of practice, which it might be well worth while reading. Their address is given at the end of the book.

Let us now consider the depth of your relationship with an advertising agent. A great deal will depend on the resources within your own organisation. If you have a marketing background yourself, or are employing somebody who has, you may feel that many of the functions normally handled by an agency can be dealt with in-house. Some agencies do everything for their clients: design the advertisements, place them, gauge the response rates, design and print all brochures, leaflets, letterheading and packaging, and handle the public relations. On the face of it this may seem like a good idea. Certainly most advertising agencies will try to persuade you to adopt this suggestion, telling you that it is the only way to obtain a cohesive and well-structured marketing plan. On the whole, we are not in favour of this. Certainly, as far as public relations is concerned, if you are going to appoint a PR consultant, and we strongly recommend that you do (see Chapter 11), then it is preferable that they should have no direct association with your advertising agency. This is because we feel there are distinct advantages to be gained by the introduction of a little healthy competition. If both your advertising agency and your PR consultants are having to share your promotional budget, they might just work that little bit harder!

This brings us on the question of your promotional material in general. If you are going into the mail order business, you need someone within your organisation who has mail order experience. This is not just our view; it is one shared by the NPA and the PPA. Let us assume, therefore, that you will be appointing somebody within your business who has a natural flair for mail order presentation – and some experience. This being the case, we would recommend that such a person should be put in charge of your brochures, leaflets and packaging. There are two main reasons for this. If you organise your brochures in-house, you will save as much as 50 per cent over what you would be charged by an agency. A direct relationship with designers, copy-writers and printers will avoid agency mark-ups. Also, when someone else is spending your money, invariably the bill ends up higher! The other factor to be taken into account is this. To be successful, mail order companies need an individual image; one which is unique to them. Agency design studios produce some wonderful work, but sometimes they are too slick, too clever; often there can be an almost clinical, impersonal aspect to their work. We are in favour of a company putting some individuality into its brochure presentation; this cannot perhaps be achieved so successfully if you turn over your entire design package to an agency. This is a tremendous generalisation of course, but even if you ignore our second point, you cannot ignore our first.

When we ran our own mail order company, we had a very good working relationship with our advertising agents – *but it was limited*. They booked all our space for us, prepared the layout of each advertisement under direction, and ensured that these layouts reached the appropriate publications on the right day. For this service they obviously charged a fee, on a piecemeal basis as well as receiving their 15 per cent. Apart from that, we did everything else ourselves. We arranged our own photography, even for advertisements, prepared our own brochures and catalogues, organised our own packaging, and used a separate PR company. Of course, we kept the agency fully informed on everything that was happening within the company. We sent them copies of all publicity material and when we held press parties they were always present. Sometimes they would attend photographic

sessions, but this was entirely voluntary on their part and no charge was made for it. About once a quarter, we would have a round-table meeting, with everyone concerned from within their company, ours and the PR agents, to discuss past, present and future promotions. Again, there was no charge. This, we feel, is the ideal relationship to have with your advertising agent. You have the benefit of all their advice, but you are not having to pay through the nose for those elements which you can perfectly well handle yourself.

There is one person on the agency staff who is all important as far as direct response advertising is concerned. It is the copy-writer. There are not many direct mail copy-writers about. Although your agency may not actually employ one, if they have mail order experience they will know of one, who may well work for them on a freelance basis. This person is vitally important to you. Ask to see his or her portfolio and, assuming you are impressed with the work produced so far, then we would strongly recommend that you use the same copy-writer throughout for all your direct response advertising.

A word on radio and television. If you are intending to experiment with direct response TV advertising, then you must have an advertising agency to negotiate the deal and provide the expertise to put together a video. There are a great many elements to TV advertising. It is not simply a question of making the right approach, nor indeed gauging the cost. There is also air time to consider, which is the subject of negotiation, and you really must deal through someone who has a thorough understanding of the media. *Again, only deal through an agency with experience.*

The same does not apply to radio. If you are a small business not wishing to employ an agency, there is nothing to stop you contacting a range of local radio stations and, as a result, making a recording to be distributed amongst them. If you already employ the services of an advertising agency, it would probably be easier for this operation to be done through them – but it is not necessary.

The same principle applies to local newspapers. If you are using your local publications for direct response advertising, you do not need to employ the services of an advertising agency. All that is necessary is for you to develop a good relationship with the newspaper sales representative and make sure that he or she stringently follows your instructions with regard to layout.

In the next two chapters of this book, we will be telling you how to put together a direct response advertisement and a brochure. Even if you do intend to employ an agency to handle all publicity material for you, it is still important that you know how to do it yourself. It must be stressed that the appointment of an advertising agency does not mean that from then on they make your decisions for you. They cannot select the products, nor calculate pricing structure, nor decide the size of your advertising budget. They are not gurus, nor a means of shelving responsibility. Remember, it is your business, your money and, ultimately, your success or failure. The buck stops firmly with you – never lose sight of that fact. An advertising agency is just one of the many mail order service industries.

7. Putting together an advertisement

Advertisements fall into two main categories: display and classified. Display can mean anything from a small double-column, black and white advertisement with no illustration, to a full-page advertisement in glorious technicolour! Obviously your first decision must be what sort of advertisement you intend to place – at least initially. Bearing in mind that classified advertising is a fraction of the cost of a reasonable-sized display, you may have no real choice, since your finances may dictate the decision. However, with the aim of helping you decide, here are a few pointers which we consider are important.

We believe that in mail order advertising your policy should be *all or nothing*. In other words, you should either take a very small classified advertisement, or a large display in full colour – the range of advertising in between is normally far from successful for direct response. Taking this idea a stage further: if you are going to be placing a classified advertisement, you will not be attempting to sell goods off the page; you will be inviting readers to send for details. Bearing in mind that this means you will have a double promotional cost – both for the advertisement and the leaflet follow-up – then it stands to reason that you will want to keep your advertising costs as low as possible. If, by contrast, you want to sell your goods via a money-off-the-page advertisement, then the bigger, the better. Certainly, as far as consumer advertising is concerned, you really should think in terms of colour. Only if you are selling a service or a concept can you afford to restrict your advertising to black and white. There is certainly black and white direct response advertising around, but this tends to fall into two categories, described below.

1. *The well-established company*. There are several companies which have been selling fashion items for years, using only black and white line drawings. They can get away with it because they have built up a following. Similarly, companies like Harrods employ this method, but, again, they have an established reputation, so that they do not have to work so hard to project an image of style and quality.

2. *The once-only advertisers*. These people try it once, but never again. Why? *Because it does not work*.

This is the age of the colour television. Full colour is what people have come to expect and, if you want to sell directly off the page, then we strongly advise you to use it. If you cannot afford to take colour advertisements, then it is far better to produce a small colour leaflet and advertise it under the classified section.

Let us now look at these two methods of advertising in greater detail.

CLASSIFIED ADVERTISING

The secret of success in a classified advertisement is the quality of your words. As you have very few to play with, every single one has to count. Your opening three or four words will make or break your advertisement. We would strongly recommend that you keep it as short as possible; the text should be no more than fifteen words at the very most. If it is too long, people lose interest.

There are certain key words which have instant appeal:

Free
Special
New
How to . . .
You can . . .
Now

Readers want to know quickly what it is that *you* can do for *them*. They are reading the classified section of the newspaper because they are looking for help, or goods, or ideas, and your advertisement must have an instant impact on them if it is to succeed. The easiest way to do this is to tell them immediately what they are going to get.

The golden rule of all promotion is to make it as easy as possible for readers to respond to your advertisement, which is why there is such a wide use of pre-paid envelopes and reply cards, with boxes to tick. People are bone lazy and if you do not make it simple they cannot be bothered to respond. With a classified advertisement you are clearly at a disadvantage in this respect. All you can do is to make your address as simple as possible. Ideally, of course, you should invest in a Post Office Freepost scheme, so that readers have only to write out an envelope, requesting details, and do not need to worry about a stamp. If you are not prepared to make this investment initially, then the next best thing is to ensure that your address is as short as possible. The most effective way to do this is to use a Post Office box number. Have a discussion with your local Post Office representative who will arrange for you to quote an address which consists only of box number, town and postcode.

It is vitally important for you to know where your inquiries have come from; the easiest way to ensure this is to add a coding to your box number. If, for example, your box number is 217, and you are placing a classified advertisement in the *Observer*, then your box number should read 217–OB1, and OB1 should apply purely to that first advertisement. Thereafter it should read OB2, OB3, etc. This arrangement is quite acceptable to the Post Office and will ensure that you not only know which newspaper or magazine is responsible for your inquiry, but which issue, too.

Although a classified advertisement by its very nature denies the possibility of any form of display, up to a point you can achieve distinction without any extra charge. Do this by insisting that some of the key words in your advertisement are in bold type and/or underlined. This will have the effect of making your advertisement stand out from the rest of the page.

This is the kind of advertisement, both in the use of words and display, which is likely to bring results:

How to learn the art of <u>YOGA</u> in the privacy of
your own home. <u>FREE DETAILS</u> from The Yoga
School, P O Box 118–OB17, Oxford OX19 3UP.

It tells the reader immediately what is on offer and how to do something about it. It is simple, straightforward, and it is playing on the fact that what is being offered is a home course in yoga, which will appeal to people who would not enjoy going out to classes – hence the words *in the privacy*. The key words YOGA and FREE DETAILS are highlighted for maximum effect.

To summarise – in classified advertising, the shorter the better, the simpler the better, the more straightforward the better.

DISPLAY ADVERTISING

Before we look at how to put together a display advertisement, it is important to be aware of the various requirements of money-off-the-page advertising.

1. The full address of the advertiser must be shown – a P O box number is not sufficient on its own. However, it is acceptable to use a box number for the coupon address, provided that your full postal address is shown elsewhere in the body copy. If a coupon is being used, then it is not enough to state even the full address on the coupon – it must be contained in the body copy of the advertisement as well.
2. The registered number of your company must be clearly displayed on the advertisement.
3. A telephone number should also be given, to which customers can refer.
4. A specific delivery period must be quoted, which should not be greater than twenty-eight days.
5. If postage and packing is to be charged, then this should be clearly stated, where ever the price is mentioned.
6. Where you are selling a product of any description, you must state the materials which have been used in manufacture.

We have advised against small display advertising, particularly black and white. However, we recognise that you may well choose to ignore us! If you are going to take a small space, try to make it stand out from the rest of the page by an imaginative border. If it is in black and white, use bold type, underlining or flashes and stars wherever you can in order to attract attention.

Case history

Years ago I (Deborah) prepared an advertisement for a client who was opening a restaurant in an old mill. We used the advertisement both in the local press and in *Yellow Pages*. It was phenomenally successful, bringing in vast numbers of people. At the time, I have to admit, I could not think why it had worked so well, until a colleague pointed it out. Because the restaurant was in a mill, I had used the idea of a mill wheel, into which I placed the copy, the result being that the advertisement was completely round. Placed among the others, more traditional in style, it stood out simply because of its shape, not because of my brilliant copy-writing as I had secretly hoped! Of course, this example was not direct response advertising, but it does indicate what you should be trying to achieve. *You need to stand out from the crowd.*

Having made our concession to small display advertising, we would once again stress that in our view it is likely to be the least successful formula. If you are going to take the plunge into display advertising, then the bigger, the better. One of the main reasons for this, apart from impact, is that you will find there is an enormous difference in your response rate if you can include a coupon within your advertising space. This has been tested again and again, always with the same results. We are back to the old chestnut: the easier you make it for your customer to order, the more likely he or she is to do so. Another factor is the position of the advertisement. A right-hand page pulls far better than a left-hand one – it is where the eye falls first. Some magazines are not prepared to guarantee right-hand pages, but try to achieve this where you can. Whether you are taking a quarter, half or full page, aim for a right-hand page and place the coupon in the bottom right-hand corner of your advertisement. If you are taking a quarter or vertical half page, try to ensure that your advertisement is placed on the outer edge of the page, so that potential customers have easy access to the coupon.

THE ILLUSTRATION

Having decided on the amount of space available after the placing of the coupon, the next priority is to ensure that your illustration is as large and as clear as possible. Avoid over-cluttering your product, particularly if you are dealing in a space allocation of less than a full page. Your aim should be to photograph the product in the best possible light and then give it as much space as you can spare. If you are taking a full page, it may be possible to include a little background, but beware of becoming over-fussy. Include nothing that will detract from the product itself.

When photographing your product, avoid black and navy. If the item is being offered in several colours, select as the major one a colour which will photograph well and then display the darker colours by means of a swatch or colour insert. For example, navy blue is the fashion houses' nightmare. As a nation, we wear a great deal of navy blue – it is possibly the most popular colour of all – but it is the very devil to photograph. A previous advertisement may have sold perhaps twice as many pairs of navy trousers as cream. So which colour should you use for the major display? Honestly, we would recommend the cream. Your customer must be able to see the detail of the products you are selling.

If you are illustrating with a drawing, again keep it simple. A good artist can display everything the customer needs to know with a few simple strokes. Too much fussy detail will make the advertisement appear muddled.

PRICE

The price should be big and bold and the very first thing you say about the product. As the reader flips through the magazine or newspaper, first his or her eye should rest on the product and then immediately on the price. Remember that if your price is subject to postage and packing, even in the display you must add in brackets afterwards 'plus p & p'.

It was Marks and Spencers who first introduced the concept that 19s 11d was more attractive than £1. Since then it has been used mercilessly in every form of retailing. One is tempted to ask, 'Why dupe the customer? Why quote £9.95? Why not simply say £10?' All one can say is that whilst the customer knows that £9.95 is virtually £10, exhaustive research shows the lower figure to be much more attractive. We have tested the alternative philosophy of rounding up items to the nearest pound – and the fact is that it simply does not work as well. There are recognisable price points – £5, £10, £20, £50, £100 – and, between these, there are less sensitive areas. In other words, if you are going to sell an item for £21.95, it probably would not greatly affect your response rate if you sold it for £22.95 instead. However, your response rate would be drastically improved if you could sell it for £19.95. If you are working in the grey areas between price points, then certainly the pound is more important than the pence. In other words, there is a difference between £26.95 and £27, but not between £27 and £27.95.

We have found the use of the word *only* is very helpful. In other words, *Only £19.95 for this cashmere sweater*, or whatever.

You will notice that we have been working in 95p rather than 99p. This is purely for arithmetical ease – both from the advertiser's point of view and the customers'. Customers make a great many mistakes on the coupon, and are far less likely to do so if they are working in fives.

BODY COPY

What you are trying to achieve in the main body copy of your advertisement is to say a great deal about what you have to sell, but in not too many words. If you look at a range of money-off-the-page advertisements, you will find they tend to fall into two categories. The page is either incredibly busy, with reams of copy, or decidedly scant, concentrating everything on making a pretty display. Frankly, we think somewhere between these extremes is the best answer. Bear in mind that your customers cannot feel or touch the product you are selling, so you need to tell them *everything* about it. Literally *every positive aspect of your product should be mentioned*. Remember, your customers need wooing!

We have suggested that the employment of a good copy-writer is a distinct advantage. However, you may decide that you would rather write the copy yourself. If this is the case, our experience suggests that informal, chatty copy works best. Certainly you want to describe the innermost workings of your product, but do not become too technical. Keep it simple, friendly and wildly enthusiastic! Above all, do not use three words where one will do. Concentrate on providing your potential customer with any information which will make the decision easier. Perhaps the most obvious example of where detail is important is in the fashion trade – it would be crazy to offer a garment for sale without a measurement chart. This equally applies to almost any product. If you are selling tables and chairs, make sure all the dimensions are included. People need to know whether the furniture will fit in the space they have available and whether it is a comfortable height. We know this all sounds very obvious, but it is surprising just how many advertisements carry incomplete details, or even totally inaccurate information. Bear in mind that if you leave out one important detail, the chances are that your response will be disastrous.

The reverse of this advice is not to be *too specific*. To take a facile example, if you are selling a waterproof garment, it would be a mistake to say that it is ideal for sailing, since non-sailors will immediately begin to feel that the waterproof is not for them. What you should be saying is that it is an ideal garment for all outdoor activities – from a leisurely walk or a round of golf to scaling Ben Nevis or crossing the Atlantic. In other words, make your catchment area of interest as wide as possible.

Finally, try to be objective about your advertising copy, whether it has been written by you or a copy-writer. Try it out on as many people as possible.

THE COUPON

As we have said, the ease with which a customer can respond to your advertisement will greatly affect your chances of success. On a practical level, your coupon should be carefully laid out so that ordering is as foolproof and as simple as possible. Head the coupon with the address to which it is to be sent and set out the order form in a box, so that the customer cannot leave out any details. If postage and packing is to be quoted as a separate item, actually print it under the total column so that it cannot get forgotten. We would strongly recommend that you offer the facility of credit cards. You must allow six to eight weeks in order to obtain credit card approval and you can make application by approaching the company direct or via your bank. The card companies will do the usual credit checks and, assuming these are satisfactory, you will find them most helpful in explaining the various procedures and supplying you with all the equipment you need. Frankly, we do not consider it essential for you to offer other card facilities – such as American Express and Diners' Club – unless your product is aimed at a business or commercial buyer. However, Barclaycard and Access really are a must.

If you are offering credit card facilities, then you should quote a telephone number which credit card holders can ring. If you are placing an advertisement in a Sunday supplement magazine or a Saturday newspaper, then this number should be usable at weekends and you should say so in the advertisement. An alternative is to operate an answerphone service, though this is not so satisfactory. This is an important point since people are becoming very conscious about ringing out of peak time and obviously they have more leisure at weekends. On the coupon you should allow not only space for the card number and symbol, but also for a signature – do leave plenty of room for the customer's address, since if this is too cramped it can cause terrible problems trying to decipher it.

As with classified advertisements, it is vital that your response is coded so that you know from where the order has been generated. If your advertisement is placed in a national newspaper, include the MOPS emblem on the coupon – it will encourage response.

In recent months, there has been a tendency for some companies to have a self-adhesive card attached to their advertisement, which can be torn off and mailed. This is taking ease of response to its ultimate conclusion, but for the extra costs involved we do not really consider it necessary.

Case history

Here is a story of how disastrously wrong direct response advertising can go, when things become over-complicated. Some years ago, working with a national Sunday newspaper, we ran a special offer for a children's corduroy jacket, jeans and matching shirt. We were acting purely as suppliers. The Sunday newspaper, therefore, was the advertiser and taking the risks.

Some advertising man somewhere dreamed up the idea of photographing the garments on children climbing a tree to rescue a cat. The children they wanted were a four-year-old girl and a nine-year-old boy.

I (Deborah) was duly summoned to Richmond Park and told to bring both clothes and children.

When I arrived, I thought we must have come to the wrong place – there were crowds of people. There was the advertising man, whose idea it was, plus his assistant, the photographer and two assistants, the cat handler, the cat, and the cat handler's assistant, a representative from the special offers department of the newspaper and her assistant – and everyone had a different view on how the shot should be taken!

I duly dressed the children. A tree had been selected and the children were hoisted up there – at least twelve feet off the ground – and the cat placed in position. There then followed a lengthy argument between the advertising man and the photographer, during which time a dog appeared from nowhere and the cat bolted, badly scratching the four-year-old on the way and causing the photographer to drop his much-prized camera. It went on like that for three hours, by which time the clothes were dirty and creased and looked dreadful. Remember, it was the clothes we were selling!

I took the exhausted children home. Twenty-four hours later I was not entirely surprised to receive a telephone call from the newspaper to tell me that the photographs were no good and that they would have to be re-shot. I threw a tantrum and said I was not putting the children through a similar experience again and it was agreed that the whole entourage should come down to Oxfordshire, so that the children could be photographed on home territory.

Believe it or not, the performance was repeated *again* – the same set of disasters, the same hoards of people, the same loss of temper . . . and goodness knows what it was all costing! Once or twice I tentatively suggested that the garments were perhaps not being shown to best advantage and I was instantly shouted down.

The second set of photographs I was told were satisfactory and three months later the advertisement appeared. It was a magnificent picture . . . of a tree. Grouped in the shadows you could just about make out two children, but the cat was nowhere to be seen, because it had been covered by the coupon – thus destroying the whole storyline! In the body copy, the newspaper forgot to mention the colourways available and, because the photograph was so dark, it was quite impossible to tell what they were. It was a full page in colour – normally costing, say, £12,000 – it took £300 worth of orders.

The salutary lesson is that if a major newspaper can make such an appalling blunder, so can we all. Everyone was so busy following the advertising man's concept, there was absolutely no room for any flexibility of thought and common sense had flown out the window. This may seem like an extreme example, but, believe us, it happens all too often.

Many a good product has failed to sell by direct response advertising, not through any design fault, nor lack of market potential, but purely because of the way in which it was displayed. Your advertisement should be simple but eye-catching; informative, yet uncluttered; individual, yet conforming to the basic rules of display; accurate, legal, convincing . . . We could cover pages with lists of appropriate adjectives. Yet if the wrong product is being displayed or the media is inappropriate, the best-designed advertisement in the world will not pull in orders. What you have to aim for is *the right product, in the right place, at the right time*. If you follow the basic rules outlined in this chapter, you should at least be in the running for a successful direct response advertisement.

8. Putting together a brochure

Initially, in the early days of your mail order operation, you need two vehicles – your main brochure, which displays most of your range of goods, and a small, cheap leaflet, displaying one or two known best-sellers and a small range of goods which are unique to the leaflet. This is how it works.

Your brochure should be sent out in the following circumstances:

1. in response to classified advertisements publicising your brochure and inviting readers to send for a copy;
2. accompanying goods being sent to customers as a result of money-off-the-page advertisements;
3. as a half yearly or quarterly mailing shot, to existing customers;
4. with goods ordered as a result of a leaflet mailing.

Your leaflet should be sent out as follows:

1. with every set of goods ordered from the main brochure;

2. as an insert in other companies' mailings, or dispatched direct to their lists;
3. as an insert in magazines or newspapers.

As your business grows, your operation will become more sophisticated. You will mail specialist leaflets to specialists sectors of your mailing list, and print leaflets to suit particular types of media. But initially the brochure/leaflet method will ensure that no goods are ever sent out without fresh literature, and that you have an opportunity to test various sorts of mail order procedure.

In this chapter we are not just looking at the brochure or leaflet, but at the whole mailing package, and we have split the various components under separate headings for ease of reference.

BROCHURE FORMAT

It is impossible to generalise about how many products you should display in your catalogue, even assuming it is a *product* you are selling, rather than a *service*. However, it has to be said that, provided the other aspects of your business can cope (that is, production, stock control, cash flow, etc.), the more items you can cram into a brochure the better. After all, give or take a few pence, it will make very little difference to printing and postage charges how many items you display, but, if the products are carefully chosen, a greater choice of goods can make a vast difference to the amount of people to whom your catalogue will appeal, and therefore to the resulting revenue.

Generally, we very much favour A5 as the ideal size of brochure. It is big enough to create a considerable impact, yet compact, easy to handle and not too weighty. Most brochures tend to be around this size, or sometimes even smaller.

Each brochure you produce should look different – and yet the same. No, this is not double Dutch. Right from the very beginning you must develop a house style. You need a logo, a standard type of printing for your company name, and one or two house colours which you always use for borders or backgrounds. This will give your brochure a familiar feel; then it is up to you to make sure that each new season looks completely different, even if a number of the same goods are being displayed because they sell so well.

As with magazines and newspapers, right-hand pages of a brochure sell the best. Funnily enough, it is not usually the front page which sells the most items, but the third – that is, the third if you count the front page as page one – so bear this in mind when allocating space. Place your winners, or potential winners, on right-hand pages, the very best on page three, and do not be afraid to enlarge the illustrations of winners out of proportion to the less saleable items. What you are aiming to do is to use every square inch of paper to maximise sales.

Your product or service may be something that does not need people to illustrate it, but we would recommend that you introduce them somewhere to give your brochure a human feel. A complete lack of people is terribly boring and leaves your brochure looking impersonal.

Even if you are sending a separate letter to customers, always have a small personal letter included in the copy of the brochure – the best place for this is page two. It should be short and sharp, and, at the very most, take up a third of a page. It should be a general message, since the brochure may be going out in a variety of different circumstances, but it should highlight the most interesting aspects of the goods available. It should be friendly and chatty, welcoming people into your brochure much as a shopkeeper would welcome customers into his shop.

A word on copy. All the points we made in *preparing an advertisement* apply equally to a brochure, except that as you will be displaying a number of items, you do need easy reference. A reference number should be shown on the photograph or illustration to clearly identify the goods; it should then precede the copy, describing that item. Make sure that the prices are shown in bold type and display one or two items which are on special offer or slightly reduced.

In the selection of your range of goods, try to make them compatible with one another. In other words, aim to lure people into buying several items rather than one by making those goods you are selling match one another, or complement one another, in some way.

Bear in mind the cost of paper and use every space available in your brochure. It is amazing how often you see brochures with a blank back page, presumably in the interests of design. It is a criminal waste of prime selling space. By contrast with an advertisement in a newspaper, you are not having to make quite the same impact to stop people turning over the page; therefore you can afford to let your brochure be somewhat more crowded than a money-off-the-page advertisement. Obviously, avoid making it confusing, but do not be afraid to cram in your products – indeed, up to a point, the more the merrier.

Now to the question of colour. Please heed our advice and print your brochure in *full colour*, even if you are selling a service. We appreciate that the full colour process is vastly more expensive than a black and white print run and we also know that a very attractive effect can be obtained by the use of coloured paper and a dashing colour ink to match it. However, it's just not good enough.

If you were advertising a restaurant situated in an old farmhouse, then a stylish leaflet in thick cream paper, overprinted in sepia, would be perfect. But you are not involved in the game of general advertising, *you are in mail order*. You are not simply trying to persuade someone to pop into your restaurant for a drink to see what it is like. You are expecting people to commit themselves to spending a sum of money on an item they have not even seen. You must show it off to best effect and you cannot achieve this result without colour – however chic the design of your brochure may be.

FORMAT

Your leaflet should be more punchy than your catalogue, altogether a harder sell. In some instances it will be going out to a less committed customer than the one who will receive your brochure and, as such, you have to work harder. Your leaflet can be quite small. One of the best we ever ran was a piece of A4 paper, folded to provide six working surfaces, one of which we used as the order form. We displayed ten different items (two per page), running the copy along the bottom – and we sold hundreds of thousands of pounds worth of goods from this one leaflet. Indeed as it carried many of our classic designs we used the same leaflet for several mailings. When we eventually changed it, we repeated the formula equally successfully.

A leaflet should be more like a money-off-the-page advertisement, in so far that is should have an immediate impact and should aim to make ordering easy for the customer. Not less than six items should be sold from a leaflet, but a dozen would be better. Do not waste space with messages to customers. Concentrate solely on displaying the goods to best possible effect, with the very minimum of good sharp copy.

Once again, our comments with regard to colour apply here.

THE ORDER FORM

Like the coupon in an advertisement, the order form should be clear and simple, with plenty of room for the customer to fill in appropriate details. It should contain your mailing address, a statement as to when delivery can be expected, the registered number of your company, and of course plenty of space for totalling the amount due, plus boxes for credit card numbers and space for the customer's signature. We would stress the need for the order form to be as foolproof as possible. It is extraordinary how people can interpret them in different ways, with the result that the wrong figures are added up or no reference numbers given. Check it again and again for ambiguity.

Make your order form an attractive piece of paper – many tend to be really uninspiring documents. Here is an opportunity to use the much-maligned single-colour process; it clearly would be crazy to use full colour on an order form. None the less, a jolly colour paper and a few flashes and stars can make it far more fun to fill in.

THE LETTER

We believe that every brochure or leaflet should be accompanied by a letter – not a personal letter to the individual customer, but a letter giving the reason for mailing the customer in the first place. If you are sending out your brochure to your regular mailing list, then the letter should take the form of a reminder as to what has happened in the past, and what the company's aims are for the future. If your leaflet is going to be inserted in, for example, the *Sunday Times*, then your letter should begin, 'As a *Sunday Times* reader . . .' In other words, you should make the customer feel that they are specially selected and not simply mailed at random.

Use the letter to highlight the best parts of your brochure or leaflet. Do not be afraid to be dramatic and fairly bullish in your approach – you are looking for immediate impact. Be relatively intimate, too, and use strong colloquial language. Keep it short, but punchy, and have it signed by whoever you have chosen to be the figurehead of your company. This is an important point, actually: customers need to be able to identify with a person, not simply a faceless company. Whether it is yourself as principal, the head of your customer relations department, your husband or wife, Joe Bloggs in Dispatch, it does not matter who, so long as there is a name to whom people can refer.

THE ENVELOPE

The envelope plays a very important part in the mail order package. How many times have you identified unsolicited mail purely by the envelope and then thrown it away without even looking at the contents? We have many, many times and we have a natural interest in mail order!

There are many different forms your envelope can take. If you are printing a reasonable quantity of brochures (10,000 plus) and are using a large printing firm, you may be able to have your brochures shrink-wrapped in polythene at the time of printing, having first supplied the printer with your customers' name and address labels to be inserted. Polythene envelopes are widely used these days and can be very attractive; and light – which helps postage costs, of course. If you leave one side of the envelope clear, the front cover of your brochure can show through, which is a very cheap form of advertising. On the whole, for a large mailing operation we would recommend this form of envelope; if your printer cannot handle the job for you, there are plenty of mailing houses who can.

The best alternative is probably a window envelope, provided you are careful to ensure that all your mailings are geared up to place the name and address in the right position. Normally the customer's name and address is printed on a self-adhesive label which, in turn, is fixed to the order form – so it is the order form layout which must be precise. These days, if you are requiring 25,000 envelopes or more, you can have them made up to your specific requirements; this often proves a more cost-effective exercise than simply buying standard envelopes off the shelf. This means, of course, that your envelopes can be made to any size.

Assuming you are mailing more than a thousand envelopes, we think it is well worth while having them over-printed with some sort of message to advertise your company. Do not print only the name and address; work out something more original. What you are trying to make your customer think is, *I must open this envelope, there is something in here which is of advantage to me*. Salesmen and -women are taught that the opening greeting to a potential customer, the firmness of their handshake, their tidy appearance are all highly relevant factors for making the initial impression which could ultimately lead to an order. Do not underestimate the impact your envelope with have on your customer, long before he or she is even aware of what you are selling.

PROMOTIONS

This is a complex area. Without doubt, promotions can make an enormous difference to customer response and, because of this, they have been vastly abused. We feel it is such an important topic that, although it is part of the brochure package, we are making it the subject of a separate chapter. See Chapter 9.

PERSONALIZATION

We hate it – or rather it would be far more honest to say we hate being the recipient of it. You know the sort of thing: 'Dear Mr Fowler, because you live at 10 St Mark's Road, you have been specially chosen . . .' etc. etc.

Surely nobody is taken in by this sort of rubbish. They must know it is nothing more than a computer exercise. A great many tests have been run on personalisation and, the fact is, as a general rule, a personalised mailing turns in a better response than a non-personalised one. None the less, the consumer is becoming increasingly aware of this form of advertising and on the whole, particularly in the early days of your mail order business, we would not recommend that you adopt it. The nearest we would suggest you get to personalisation is with regard to pre-printing the customer's name and address on the order form – as we have suggested if you intend using a window envelope. This is quite a useful device as it does plant in the customer's mind the idea that he or she is expected to place an order. It also speeds up the order processing, since the name and address will be clearly decipherable.

Once your business is established, then probably it would be sensible to test personalisation on a small batch of customers. It does need to be recognised, with the increasing sophistication of technology, that eventually customers will be treated in a completely individual way, exactly as though they had walked into their local store. However, in the meantime, mass-produced personalisation, in our view, leaves a lot to be desired and should not be placed at the top of your priority list.

So, these are the main aspects you should consider in the preparation of your brochure. Make sure that you adhere to the variety of legislation that surrounds direct mail – it all makes sense. After all, you should be doing everything you can to make your potential customers feel reassured. You need to anticipate every question they will ask themselves, just as if you were having a conversation with them – and make sure those questions are answered in full.

Ultimately you need to ask yourself whether your brochure is an attractive thing to read? Do you turn the pages with pleasure? It sounds as though we are expecting a lot – and we are. Think of the tens of thousands of pounds which are spent on shop displays and prestige showrooms. These are fulfilling exactly the same role as your brochure – it is a showroom for your merchandise. How easy would it be to sell a Rolls-Royce from a corrugated shed with a leaking roof? Would a diamond ring look as good if it were not displayed in a velvet lined box? No, of course not. Bear these thoughts in mind when you set about producing your first brochure.

9. Promotions

Free gifts, prize draws, lotteries, games of chance, even contests of skill – all these are devices used by mail order companies to persuade their would-be customers to order more, or indeed order at all. There has been a considerable amount of bad publicity over the last few years with regard to promotions. It is also true to say that quite a number of promotions have backfired, causing more ill feeling than goodwill.

A prime example of bad promotion is where a customer receives a letter telling him that he has been specially selected to be entered for a prize draw, the first prize being, shall we say, £100,000. In order to qualify for this selection process, of course, the customer has to place an order to a certain minimum value. This he does and then never hears another word. He is neither advised when, or where, the draw is taking place, nor, to his knowledge, is a list of prize winners ever published. The result of all this is that the customer believes he has been duped and that in fact no draw has ever taken place. Sometimes his fears are justified.

We have already advised you to write to the Advertising Standards

Authority, to acquire their booklet *The British Code of Advertising Practice*. The ASA have also produced *The British Code of Sales Promotion Practice*. You will find their address at the end of the book.

The ASA promotion booklet is a very good publication. It is easy to read and detailed in explanation. Clearly there is no point in our reproducing it here, but there are one or two points we feel it is particularly worth summarising.

Take the issue of free gifts. As a company providing a free gift to your customer, in response to an order of a certain value, it is important that you have the right attitude towards that gift. Even though it is *free*, the gift is still subject to all the conditions under which you supply goods for which the customer has paid. In other words, the free gift must comply in terms of quality, colour and size with the description you have given. It must be dispatched within twenty-eight days and, if it is faulty, it must be replaced. Inevitably there is a tendency amongst mail order traders to take a rather cavalier approach to their free gifts. 'We are giving the customer something for nothing, so he has no cause for complaint,' is a not untypical attitude. Certainly, one or two companies with whom we have been involved have dispatched to their customers the most appalling junk as free gifts, which bore absolutely no relation to the alluring description of the items the customers were told they would receive. If this is your attitude, then we feel sure you are doing your company more harm than good by offering a free gift at all. Remember, too, that by promising to dispatch a gift in response to an order, you have made that gift a condition of sale. If the gift is not up to scratch, you could be sued – and successfully.

The other major point to consider is the need to present very clear and precise rules and conditions in the event of your running a competition or draw. It is a legal requirement, in any event, but another consideration is that customers do become very upset if they are not told the full facts. What do we mean by rules and conditions? It needs to be spelt out when the closing date occurs for the competition, whether you can apply if you live outside the United Kingdom or are under eighteen, the date on which judges will be making their decision, and when prize winners will be notified. It is all very obvious, but terribly important in order to reassure the customer that you are running a bona fide promotion. Remember, the whole object of a promotion is to create goodwill. You can only do this if you are scrupulously fair and straightforward in your dealings – and seen to be so.

Case history

A large, rich, ageing friend of ours has bought clothes from a specialist mail order company for some years. Last season, for the first time, the company in question employed promotion techniques. They wrote to our friend Mary and told her that, as she was a valued customer, if she sent in her order before a particular date she would receive a free gift and her name would be put forward for the prize draw worth £50,000. Mary complied and then there was a complete silence. After a while, she wrote asking about her free gift. Her letter was not acknowledged. Incensed, she wrote to the managing director, demanding her free gift and asking for full details of the prize draw. The managing director replied, saying that her letter had been passed to the promotions department, who would be in touch with her shortly. Again, a long silence. Finally, unbelievably angry now, Mary asked her solicitor to write to the company and only on receipt of a solicitor's letter did a free gift arrive and a relatively satisfactory letter explaining that the prize draw had taken place and the prize winners notified. Mary was not amongst them.

Mary's solicitors wrote direct to the prize winners and established that they had all received their prizes, which proved the company was not acting in a fraudulent way – they were simply being thoughtless. Perhaps Mary over-reacted, but in her mind she had entered into a contractual agreement with the company: if she sent them her order within a specified period, she would receive something in return. When she did not, she was understandably angry.

The upshot of all this is that Mary is still hopping mad about the whole incident. She would have placed that order anyway, because she has bought from the company every season for years. She is becoming increasingly housebound and so is more dependent on mail order purchasing than she used to be – and she has no shortage of cash. However, she is adamant that she will never buy from the company again. So much for promotions!

So we have looked at what can happen when things go wrong. How about when they go right? Is there really any value in sales promotion? Certainly, according to a number of major mail order companies, who automatically run promotional schemes with every new brochure. They are adamant that a promotion, linked to order value or quick response, does have very good results. We cannot help thinking, though, that some of these promotions are becoming rather over-complicated and much too elaborate. When I (Deborah) ran my own mail order company, I used a very simple device. With every brochure I sent out to our main mailing list, I included a £1 voucher. Customers were told that if their order value exceeded £25 and was received by a certain date, they could deduct £1 from the total cost of the goods. I firstly tested this on a random mailing list of 10,000, out of a total mailing of 35,000. The orders from the 10,000 were 11 per cent up in terms of total expenditure, and thereafter I adopted the scheme for all my main catalogue mailing shots. Perhaps it would have been even better if I had offered a £100,000 prize draw, but I am not at all sure that this would have been the case – and in any event, I could not afford it!

Undoubtedly, people do like something for nothing. If your promotion can be linked to quick response – that is, orders have to be received within a certain period – this does help counteract the inertia factor. If a potential customer does not order immediately upon receipt of the brochure, there is a tendency for it to be stuffed in a drawer and forgotten. This is far less likely to happen if there is a positive advantage to be gained from ordering quickly.

So treat promotions with respect, or, rather, *treat your customers with respect*. Do not make promises, however trivial, unless you are prepared to keep to them; read carefully the legal implications outlined in the Advertising Standards Authority booklet on promotions; and remember the main object of a promotion – *to build goodwill*.

10. Direct mail production: a guide to the world of printing

In order to make the most of a direct mail operation, you need to acquire a thorough understanding of the printing world. You need to be able to talk intelligently to typesetters, designers, copy-writers and printers themselves. You need to understand what is meant by artwork, colour reproduction, galley proofs, dummies, bleeds, origination and a host of other terminology. This chapter is not intended to explain the pros and cons of sending out a mail shot – that comes later. Here we are concerned purely with printed matter in order to ensure that you have your first brochure printed against a background of a good all-round knowledge of the trade.

The production process of your brochure, from start to finish, will take four to five months. There are ten stages of brochure production and along the way there are inevitable hold-ups, so really four months is the very minimum you should allow. If your brochure is a biannual event this obviously gives you a degree of breathing space. If, however, you are going to produce three or more brochures a year, you can see that you will always have one at some stage of development.

The ten stages of brochure production are given below.

1. The selection of products and ordering of photographic samples
2. Preparation of a design layout
3. Photography
4. Selection of photographs and re-photographing where necessary
5. Copy-writing
6. Artwork
7. Colour reproduction
8. Correction of proofs
9. Printing
10. Distribution

The above procedure applies whether you are printing 5,000 brochures or 500,000, and before you begin any work on your brochure you need to produce two schedules – a cost analysis and a production chart.

COST ANALYSIS

Each element of your direct mail costs should be itemised and then set against your budget figure. Initially, of course, the analysis will include such items as your photography and artwork costs and, ultimately, all mailing expenditure including postage. What you should be aiming to do is to calculate a figure which represents the actual cost of each brochure, so that this information, together with your response rate, will enable you to assess the profit or loss on each mailing.

PRODUCTION CHART

The ten stages should be plotted on a chart, showing dates on which each should be completed. Printers, like builders, have quite a reputation for getting behind on schedules and you need a very clear idea of when each stage will be completed so that you can quickly chase up any delays.

For ease of reference, we have divided up the production process under a series of headings.

FINDING A PRINTER

Although printing is near the end of the chain, the selection of a printer will affect everything else you do, so it is where you should begin. There is the question of size. If your print run is small, that is, up to 5,000, you should be thinking in terms of a local printer – not too large – someone to whom you will be important. For print runs of 10,000 plus you can start looking a little further afield; over 100,000, frankly you should feel free to choose a printer anywhere in the country if you consider their operation is right for you.

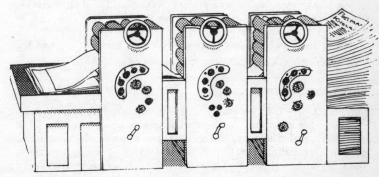

When it comes to the selection of your printer, never be satisfied with discussing your requirements with a salesperson. They are there to take orders. You need to establish a relationship with the production people. To this end we would strongly recommend that you visit the print works and discuss your requirements with the managing director – whatever your size of print run. Let's face it, if you are going into mail order, you are going into the print business, and one day your orders could be worth a great deal of money. If a printing firm is too short-sighted to see this, then they are not going to offer you the best in terms of quality of service.

Be particularly careful about sub-contracting. It is a difficult business being a printer – their main aim is to keep their machines running; often, in order to achieve this, they take on more business than they can handle. When this happens, they simply sub-contract out that part of the work they cannot manage. You need to make it quite clear that this is not going to happen to *your* brochure. Visit the premises and take a careful look around the print works. Is it neat and tidy? Does the place have a look of quiet efficiency about it, or do you suspect they are working in a state of controlled (or uncontrolled) chaos? In mail order, precise and reliable delivery is vital. If you suspect a printing firm might be unreliable, do not touch it with a barge pole – there are plenty of others around.

Make sure you take up references. A good printer will be only too pleased to supply you with the names of one or two regular customers. It may be that you select your printer by personal recommendation in the first place. Certainly we would strongly recommend that you should not place your printing requirements with anyone on whom you can run no check.

The other consideration in the selection of a printer is the type of printing process being used. Printing is no longer the straightforward business it used to be and there are a number of different processes relevant to mail order.

Letterpress

This is the traditional method of printing, whereby paper is fed through rollers, which press raised images on to it. These days letterpress is used mostly in magazine, newspaper and book production. The great advantage of letterpress is that it gives you enormous flexibility. It is quite easy to make alterations during the print run. The main disadvantages are that it is a slow process and the cost of plates is higher than for most of the alternatives.

Offset lithography

Litho machinery can vary enormously – from really very small printing presses to the enormous Webb offset machines which can print at an incredible speed. The principle is that the areas of paper which require no print are chemically treated so that the ink does not adhere to the surface. The main advantages of offset litho are that it is relatively inexpensive, it prints very fast and is very versatile with regard to the different types of paper that can be used. It is ideal for a long, uncomplicated run, but if alterations have to be made it is expensive, as any corrections require the making of a completely new plate.

Silk screen

The printing process here is rather like a stencil. It is good for one-off jobs – anything from posters to T-shirts. The colours always come out very bright and the process is particularly suitable for very small jobs requiring considerable impact. It is definitely not suitable for long runs.

Gravure

This process involves the ink being brought up under pressure, literally sucked on to the surface of the paper; this type of printing is ideal for prestige work. If a really top-quality job is required – beautiful printing on first-class paper – then gravure is your process. The cost of plates is high and so we would not recommend it for short runs. In general, it is not really ideal for mail order.

Laser printing

This has to represent a great move forward in technology. A laser beam searches out the image to be printed and then transfers it on to the paper by heated roller. This process is ideally suited for personalised literature and indeed great advances are being made all the time. It is felt that this has to be the ideal mail order printing method of the future.

Having selected your printer, your next task is to decide whether he or she should handle the whole job for you or only the actual printing process. Assuming you already have a rough layout and photographs, where appropriate, you can either ask the printer to handle the artwork and colour reproduction or you can deal direct with the people offering these services. If you have a small run – 5,000 or less – then it would be better to let your printer handle everything for you. However, if your print run is over 10,000, we would suggest you should shop around and try to make these relationships direct. After all, when a printer offers these services, he or she is certainly marking up the price being charged to him or her. Be careful, though: both processes are vital. It is important to find somebody on whom you can rely.

The relationship you form with your printer should not be looked on as a lifelong commitment. As your business develops, your printing requirements will change and, in any event, staying with one supplier will have a tendency to make that person complacent and therefore less competitive.

You are likely to find that it will be sensible to have your order form printed in a different place from your brochure. Order forms are best dealt with on a letterpress machine, which will give the flexibility for coding. Your brochure is more likely to be printed on an offset litho machine or by laser printing. Insist that all the printers you approach put their quotations in writing and insist also on a written delivery date. Their ability to deliver on time will be conditional upon their receiving artwork and/or colour reproduction by a certain date. Allow a little flexibility here, since inevitably there will be the odd hiccup and you do not want to give your printer an excuse for being late.

DESIGN WORK

The design of your brochure falls into two distinct parts.

The rough

A rough layout must be produced once you have selected which products you are going to include in your brochure. This rough will be used for a number of purposes. First, it will form the basis upon which you obtain quotations from printers, colour reproduction houses and artists for final artwork. Second, presenting the rough to your photographer will enable him or her to see the shape of the photographs you require. You should take time and trouble planning your rough and it is essential this is done before any attempt is made to photograph the products.

Some people design their own roughs, but it is almost certainly better to use a professional artist, who could be somebody employed by your advertising agency or recommended by your printer. Whoever the artist is, it is important that you establish a good working relationship and that he or she has a flexibility of thinking that enables him or her to incorporate your ideas, rather than exclusively following his or her own ones. Make sure the balance between illustration and copy is correct and try to ensure that each double-page spread looks different, so that as one leafs through the brochure, each spread makes a separate impact. A border round each page is a good idea, as taking the illustration right to the edge of the paper is expensive. In any event, an attractive border helps to make a page look good.

The artwork

The second stage of design is the artwork. Artwork, or camera-ready artwork, as it is usually called, is what you will be presenting to your colour reproduction house or printer, depending on your use of colour and who is handling it. The person who prepares your artwork might well be the same artist who designed the rough – in fact this is preferable. You will need to present that person with your copy, which should be carefully typed to minimise error, and your photographs, indicating how much of the photograph you want – you may require some of the background to be cut out.

On your copy you should indicate very clearly the headings and how large you want them; where colour is being used, you should advise the artist what colour borders, type and backgrounds you require. Strictly speaking, this information can be passed direct to your colour reproduction people, but it is far safer to have the information written on the artwork so that no mistakes can be made during colour reproduction.

The first thing your artist will do is to have your copy typeset in the type of your choice, so that he or she can see how it will fit on to the page. The artist will then pass the type to you for checking. These proofs will usually come to you in the form of a long strip of type, with no attempt at layout. It is not the layout that is important at this stage. What is vital is that you check the proofs very carefully, correcting all typographical mistakes. Remember that the further along the production line you go, the more expensive and difficult it is to make alterations. Take time and trouble with your corrections.

Once the page layouts are drawn up, the type will be pasted down in position. Before your artwork is finally handed over to you, the artist should go through it with you, providing a photostat copy on which you can mark corrections. Again, take care – alterations at this stage cost next to nothing. At the colour reproduction stage they can be horrendously expensive.

COLOUR REPRODUCTION

Colour reproduction involves the making of colour negatives. Full colour illustrations are made up by the use of four sets of tiny dots in the primary colours – red, blue, yellow and black. A separate negative is made for each colour, having first scanned the colours in your photographs to achieve the right mix. In selecting the people to do your colour reproduction, ask to see some of their work, for quality is very important here. The fact is that if the reproduction is badly done the printer will not be able to produce a work of quality.

When you present your artwork to the colour reproduction people, it is sensible to provide them with some colour samples to support your photographs. In other words, if you are selling books, bringing along the book jackets would help enormously so that they can make sure the colour is as accurate as possible. There is a considerable amount of manoeuvrability with colour reproduction which can prove to be both a disadvantage and an advantage. If you are not vigilant, the colours can end up quite different from your photograph. If can be useful, however. Once we had a fabric crisis and were able to change the photograph of a bottle-green dress to a maroon dress during the colour reproduction stage!

Your colour reproduction house will provide you with colour proofs. Ask for plenty and show them around to as many people as possible. Normally your proofs will come on sheets of A2 paper, containing a number of different pages. It is well worth while cutting up the pages and putting them together so that you can see how the brochure will look when it is bound. At this stage, as well as checking the accuracy of the colour, you will also find that there are a number of splodges and dots which have somehow found their way on to the negatives. All these must be marked on the proofs so that they can be removed before the job is finally handed over to the printer. Where the colour is wrong it is quite possible to put it right at this stage. However, once the job is on the printing press, although colour can be adjusted, it is difficult to do so in a localised area. Where, for example, something blue might have too much red in it, you can remove a little red during the printing process, but it will affect the whole double-page spread and may make some other item look insipid. So make your comments on colour *now*.

PAPER

The quality of the paper you use for your brochure is a very important consideration. Paper represents approximately 50 per cent of the printing cost and so you will appreciate that the type of paper you choose to use will make a vast difference to the price quoted to you by your printer. This is an important point. When you are comparing one printer's quotation with another's, do make sure that you are comparing like with like and that the variation in price is not simply a question of different qualities of paper. Printing on too cheap a paper can be a false economy. The better the paper, the better your photographs will look; good-quality paper suggests that your products will be good quality too. We have all received catalogues through the post where the paper is cheap and flimsy, little better than newsprint; the photographs tend to be smudged and indistinct. This has to be wrong. However, you must be sure to consider the weight of your paper. A better-quality paper could well put you from one postage bracket into a higher one, and when you are sending out a large mailing shot, this is a crucial factor as far as your costs are concerned. Our advice is to use the best quality of paper you can, given your resources and your postages costs.

Always print your catalogue on standard-size paper. This does not mean that catalogues have to end up looking a standard size, since paper can be folded in a number of different ways. As a guide, in the table we list the standard paper sizes. The measurements quoted refer to the paper when trimmed. As it is supplied to the printer, it is slightly larger.

Standard paper sizes

Sizes	Millimetres
A0	841 × 1,189
A1	594 × 841
A2	420 × 594
A3	297 × 420
A4	210 × 297
A5	148 × 210
A6	105 × 148
A7	74 × 105
A8	52 × 74
A9	37 × 52
A10	26 × 37

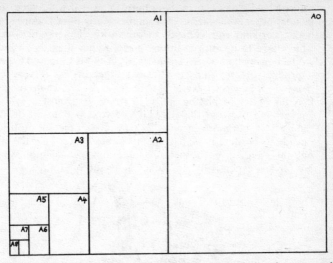

Some large mail order houses do not leave it to their printer to order paper, but form a direct relationship with a paper mill. This can save money, but we would suggest it is not something that you should consider until you are dealing in very large print runs.

Do not forget coloured paper. Coloured paper is more expensive that white, but in some instances it is cheaper to use a coloured paper than print a background colour.

A FEW HELPFUL HINTS

1. *Copy*. As a general rule, always print your copy in black. There are two reasons for this. First, copy is the one aspect of your brochure you are most likely to want to change and it is far cheaper and easier to change a black plate than the others. Second, without a doubt, black print has the best definition and is the most easy to read.

2. *Background colour*. Do be careful not to make your background colours too dark. They should be a light wash of pastel colour, nothing stronger. If the background is too dark, it detracts from the products you are selling and also it can be very difficult to print. If, for example, you placed your photographs in a dark navy surround, there would be a tendency for such a density of blue to affect the complexions of the people in your photographs, making them slightly dirty in appearance. Good printers can sometimes avoid this, but it is better to steer clear of the problem altogether.

3. *Cut-outs*. Advertising agencies in particular are mad keen about cut-outs. This is where an individual figure or a product is lifted off its natural photographic background and placed over the

printed background in the brochure. You will have seen this process often in magazines. Sometimes the cut-out is done very badly; certainly is is difficult to cope with elements like hair, which have to be cut out in one piece, rather than on an individual hair-by-hair basis. An enlarged cut-out is supposed to give a product greater impact. However, the process is very expensive – it may cost several hundred pounds. We would suggest it is far better to photograph your products against a neutral background to avoid this necessity. If you want to create the same effect, but more cheaply, let part of your picture protrude outside its border, as we have demonstrated here. Like the cutout, this device gives the picture a three-dimensional impression, but far less expensively and rather more subtly.

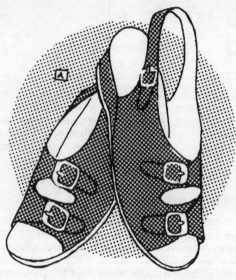

4. Always avoid dates in your brochure. If it is successful, you may find yourself using it again and again over quite a protracted period. Even if you do not use the whole brochure, you may repeat certain pages in future promotion material. If, for example, you wish to offer some form of incentive for a quick response, always use the order form or a separate letter to give details of the scheme – *never, never the brochure*.

5. Always attend the print run, even if it is at three o'clock in the morning, which it all too often is! Once your brochure is up on the machine, the printer will run through a number of copies to check the colour and make sure all is well. Be there to see those copies come off the machine – it is a fascinating process anyway and far from unenjoyable. Your insistence on being present not

only is sensible, but it also demonstrates to the printer that he or she has got to handle your job with care. If your printer has also been responsible for the colour work, it is possible, on a small run, that you may not have seen colour proofs before the actual printing process. In this event, it is absolutely vital that you are there as the job comes off the machine.

6. In Chapter 16 we will be discussing the pros and cons of using a mailing house to dispatch your brochures. If you *are* going to use a mailing house, do make sure you tell them the exact format of your brochure before it is printed. The chances are that the mailing house you use will have collating machines for sending out mail shots and it is important that your brochure fits their system. Similarly, when it comes to transporting your brochure from printer to mailing house, check with the mailing house as to how they would like the brochures packed and in what sort of quantity – in other words, anything to make the job easier for them. Remember that these comments apply not just to the brochure but also to the order form, letter and envelopes you use.

7. As already discussed in Chapters 7 and 8, it is very important to be able to gauge your response rate from your various different mailing sectors. The only way you can do this is to code your order form. Obviously when working out your total print run you will have already decided where your brochure is to be mailed. If you provide your printer with a series of codes, these can be changed during the printing process to your specifications.

8. Assuming you are having a reasonably large print run, say, over 50,000, it would be useful to conduct one or two tests. Try swapping your pages around, particularly page three, to see how the sale of products varies according to where they are placed in the brochure. To achieve this, all you have to do is to ensure that your page numbers are printed in black and then you can ask the printer to change the page numbers half-way through the print run. This has to be done very carefully, but should involve very little extra cost provided you move whole spreads at a time.

9. Always print more order forms than brochures. Customers are always asking for extra order forms and you may wish to include one when dispatching goods.

Finally we thought it would be helpful if we listed some of the printing terminology, with a brief description as to what each means. These words tend to be banded around and to the uninitiated, it can all sound very confusing.

Bleeds   This is where the printing of an illustration is taken right up to the edge of the paper so that there is no border. It involves the printer buying slightly larger paper than he or she would normally do and printing well over the trimming line. It is expensive but it can be very effective with certain illustrations.

Dummy   This is a useful device to give your printer when you hand over your artwork. You should take photostats of you artwork, trim and paste it together, and fold it precisely as you want your finished brochure to look. This will enable the printer to see exactly what you are aiming for. The dummy is particularly useful if you are involved in any sort of complicated folding, for example, in the case of a reply paid card.

Folio   Folio is the word used for page numbers.

Format   This is the word used to describe the physical appearance of your total mailing package, for instance, your brochure, envelope, letter, order form.

Galley proofs   This is the name given to the first proof you will receive from the typesetter. The proof will take the form of long strips of typing where no attempt has been made at layout. Its purpose is to check for typographical errors.

Keying   This is the term used to describe the code you use on your order form to identify different mailings. The different codes are referred to as key changes.

Origination   This is the term used to describe whatever it is you hand over to the printer, whether it is artwork or partially finished artwork, or colour negatives from the reproduction house. In other words, it is the point at which the printer sets to work.

Out of register   This is the term used to describe that dreadful 'double vision' effect that you see all too often in mail order printing. It is caused by one or more of the plates becoming out of alignment during the printing process. If your brochure is printed out of register, it should be reprinted free of charge. If your advertisement is printed out of register, you should receive a substantial rebate. Either way, you are likely to be told the cause is your photographs not being sharp enough. Don't stand for it!

Scamp   This is purely an outline sketch of the brochure layout, showing nothing more than headings and the odd indication as to how the end product will look. The positioning of the copy is roughly sketched in, but there are usually no words, simply a series of wiggles to show where they should go.

Rough   A rough is one stage on from a scamp. It will show precisely where the copy and illustrations are to be placed and there will be a certain degree of copy heading. A rough will be sufficient for a printer to quote on, or a photographer to use for taking the shots.

We hope this chapter has been helpful in making you feel slightly at home in the printing world. Do not underestimate the importance of understanding the process, because your printed matter is your shop window. The degree of professionalism with which you produce your brochure and associated literature will not just influence the degree of response, it could be the difference between make or break as far as your business is concerned. Be organised, know precisely where you are on timing. Check and recheck every price, every detail of copy and, if you do not understand a process, ask for it to be explained to you. We have given you a superficial knowledge, but now, quite literally, you need to go and smell the ink and feel the paper! The kind of printer you want to find is someone who is going to take the time and trouble to explain to you what he or she is doing, and why. Your printer's business is your business now. If he or she is not prepared to give you plenty of help and guidance, then find someone who will.

11. Public relations: its value to the mail order business

The most successful advertisement we ever ran was in a Sunday supplement, late in January 1979. January is not a good month to advertise. We were somewhat sceptical about going ahead, but because there were few advertisers about we were quoted a very good rate and it was too tempting an offer to refuse.

Some weeks previously, we had been interviewed by the newspaper section of the same publication. We knew the article was going to appear some time, but we were told probably not until March. Instead, they found a slot in the main newspaper in the same weekend as our advertisement appeared in the supplement. The result was quite extraordinary. Sales were out of all proportion to anything we had come to expect, despite the time of year. This one example demonstrates the extraordinary power of public relations.

In the eyes of the public, all advertising is biased, however clever or spectacular. *You* are telling the world how wonderful *you* are. Not so with public relations – a journalist recommending your product is worth a ton of advertising, for this represents *someone else* saying how wonderful you are.

Public relations is often not even considered by the small business person. To that person, it is representative of the sort of window dressing used by large companies, rather than a vehicle which can make a serious contribution to business development. There is a tendency to think that PR has no role to play apart from building your business image, but good publicity can have far more tangible effects than that. We would go so far as to say that if you are intending to launch a mail order business, then PR is a must.

When we began our business, we undertook our own PR. This largely took the form of visiting all appropriate magazines and newspapers, by appointment, and delivering a copy of our catalogue. Where it appealed to journalists, they would write a piece of editorial, advising their readers that our new catalogue was available and sometimes printing a photograph of our goods. The trick is to persuade the journalist to quote the address of your company so that readers can send direct for a catalogue. On the whole, journalists are prepared to do this – otherwise they are inundated with inquiries. As a list-building exercise, this is an excellent method of obtaining publicity and, of course, above all, it is *free*!

A very well-known columnist in one of the Sunday newspapers used to regularly report on our new catalogue and she always quoted our address. She never gave us a great deal of space, no more than five or six centimetres of a single column, plus a small line drawing, but we used to receive between 2,000 and 3,000 inquiries as a result. We dread to think how much advertising we would have had to invest in to achieve the same results.

PR for mail order does not stop with editorial mention. Once our business was well established, we began employing a small firm of PR consultants and they introduced us to the world of competition and sponsorship, mainly through the provincial press. This is how it works. Through a local paper, or paper group, you plan a simple competition and you donate prizes in the form of a voucher to buy goods from your catalogue to a certain value. The prizes do not have to be huge – the first prize needs be no more than, say, £35. Readers then take part in the competition, send in their order forms, and the winners are selected.

Now, here is the good news: in most cases the newspaper will be prepared to give you *all* the names of the competitors. By inference, these names represent people who are interested in your product or they would not have bothered to enter the competition – so, suddenly, you have a ready-made mailing list. The provincial press is very often under estimated. Some local newspapers have enormous circulations, bigger even than the nationals, and their pulling power is considerable. Bearing in mind that the very nature of your business involves national distribution, you can afford to sponsor these competitions literally anywhere in the country.

A good way to make the public more aware of your company and its products is to consider syndicated articles, either through provincial press or local radio. You invite a journalist to interview you on a subject which you consider to be of general interest and which is closely linked to your own products. Where newspapers are concerned, the resulting interview is typed up, packaged with black and white photographs and distributed around the country. A good ready-made story, complete with illustrations, will be taken up by a number of publications. As far as radio is concerned, more or less the same thing applies. You make a taped interview and distribute the tape around local radio stations.

Once you employ PR consultants, you should consider a press party once a year to launch your new catalogue. Thousands of pounds are lavished on these affairs, with floor shows, expensive free gifts, sometimes even trips abroad, all geared to persuade journalists to cover the story. We found a room in a decent hotel, handy to Fleet Street, from where we dispensed gallons of plonk and a cold buffet. This was quite sufficient to do the trick! Journalists are busy people, so your party needs to be close to their offices, at lunchtime (but not on a Friday) – and boozy. If your product is worth mentioning, this sort of party will do the trick! Do get your PR consultants to handle the details for you – things like the timing of the invitations are absolutely critical.

The art of good PR is finding something newsworthy to say about your business. If you are a small new company, the mere fact that you are a struggling entrepreneur will be enough for the first story. Thereafter journalists will be looking for a different angle. Each season you should think in terms of a new product or theme which will lend itself to PR. You might even go so far as to produce one or two products specifically geared to this. Contrary to popular belief, it is not difficult to appeal to journalists. Indeed they are always looking for fresh material. Make sure you are on the alert to seize opportunities as they arise. Perhaps something comes up in the news which is of relevance to you and your business, in which case, act fast – yesterday's news is no use at all. Certainly the more coverage you can get, the easier you will find it to promote your company; this is the chicken-and-egg syndrome again. Once the media have accepted you as being newsworthy, you will find that from time to time they are quite likely to approach you, and now and again a situation may crop up which will give you a lucky break. For example, I (Deborah) was working as a freelance consultant for Damart when Princess Diana was asked how she managed to look so warm and cheerful on her walkabouts when everyone else around her was freezing. Damart thermal underwear was her secret, she confided. What a story, a PR consultant's dream! These sort of breaks do happen from time to time – though this is particularly dramatic example.

HANDLING YOUR OWN PR

In the early days of your mail order business, it could be a good idea to handle your own PR. Because of the difficulties the industry has experienced in recent years, the press are a little suspicious of mail order companies, particularly those who have no retail outlets. Being taken out to lunch by the managing director, being given the offer to come and see round your works, can do a great deal towards reassuring the journalist that you are a bona fide organisation. Every journalist dreads the idea of writing an article about a company whose product or service turns out to be an absolute disaster – as a result of which hundreds of readers lose their money.

We would suggest that you begin by circulating your catalogue, but do make sure you do so *before* it is released to your customers. One of the reasons for recommending that you ask your printer for plenty of proofs (as suggested in Chapter 10) is for this very purpose. Journalists like the idea of having something hot off the press; they are certainly going to be less interested in a brochure which has been dispatched already. This is particularly true if you are involved in a seasonal trade such as fashion.

With your brochure it is sensible to produce what is known as a 'press release'. This should take the form of a single sheet of paper on which you have outlined the main points of interest with regard to your brochure. It speeds things up from a journalist's point of view – and you can use it to highlight some of the details about your business which are not included in the catalogue. Always make sure that you have black and white photographs of your most newsworthy lines, of yourself, your premises and your staff at work. Always make sure, too, that you have samples of your products available for inspection. Familiarise yourself with the press by reading all publications which could be relevant to you, so that you get to know the style of the various columnists and feature writers. Do not feel inhibited about making an approach, nor imagine your business is unlikely to be of interest. Make it interesting. What is routine work to you could be a fascinating insight into another industry to someone else.

SELECTING A PR CONSULTANT

At some time during the development of your business, you will need a PR consultant to take over the day-to-day public relations exercise. This does not mean that you opt out of the role altogether. In fact quite the contrary: every PR campaign needs a central figure who can be available for interview. However, PR is time-consuming and at some stage you will need to recognise that it is taking up too much of your energy.

The best way to find a reputable firm of public relations consultants is to contact the Institute of Public Relations, whose address is given at the end of the book. They will give you a complete list of PR consultants and will be pleased to advise you as to the type of business each firm services. Like advertising agents, in our view it is preferable that they are London-based, since they tend to have closer relationships with the journalists if they are local to Fleet Street; and that they have at least one other client who is in mail order. They need to understand the business in order to represent it properly.

Another source of information on PR consultants is a directory called *The Hollis Press and Public Relations Annual*. This can be obtained from the address listed at the end of the book.

Most public relations firms will ask for a monthly retainer, plus expenses. Compared with the sort of advertising budget you will be looking at, the sum involved is fairly small, but, unlike advertising, you cannot expect immediate results. PR takes time – time to establish contacts with journalists, time before articles are actually published, and time before a gradual build-up of exposure starts to have any tangible effect on your business. In our view there is very little point in undertaking a PR campaign which is going to run for less than a year, unless, of course, you are specifically wanting to promote one single event.

In order to obtain the very best service from your PR consultant, here are a few points which we consider useful.

1. Keep your PR consultants fully informed as to *all* your company's activities. As mentioned earlier, journalists are always looking for a fresh angle to a story. Some aspect of your business development which may seem comparatively minor to you could make a wonderful piece of editorial copy. So do keep your PR consultants briefed on any changes or developments in your business, however insignificant they may seem to you.

2. Provide your PR consultants with good service – in other words make sure they have all your up-to-date catalogues, brochures and leaflets, a stock of black and white and colour photographs and a selection of samples from your latest product range. Journalists operate in a strange way. Everything happens at the last minute. This may be because a story has suddenly become newsworthy, or because a blank column needs filling urgently. Either way, you can be confident that every story will be the subject of a last-minute panic.

    Your PR consultants may have been pursuing a particular journalist for months. Suddenly, one day, he will ring up demanding photographic samples the same afternoon and saying that the only time he can interview you is ten o'clock that night. This may seem somewhat inconsiderate, not to mention inconvenient, but you have to play the game. Whatever you are doing – forget it. Move heaven and earth to comply with their wishes. A good interview in a national newspaper could provide an enormous shot in the arm for your business, not to mention your mailing list!

3. This brings us on to the next point. PR consultants need your personal backing. Indeed many journalists are simply not prepared to talk to a PR man or woman; they want to speak direct to the company. *You* are your best ambassador. No one can talk about your business with as much conviction and flair as you can. Even if you have never been interviewed in your life before, it is surprising how quickly you can become used to talking on radio

or television, or to magazines and newspapers. If you feel unable to cope with this yourself, then you must nominate somebody from within your company in a senior position to handle this aspect for you.

4. Never allow any of the media to promote a product which you do not have readily available. It is the kiss of death as far as your future PR prospects are concerned. As we have already mentioned, dissatisfied readers are every journalist's nightmare. If a piece of editorial coverage generates considerable interest in your product, *you must be able to fulfil that interest – fast*.

5. If you are embarking on a PR campaign, make sure that you or your PR consultants take out a press-clipping service. There are a number of companies who specialise in this. It is their job, for a comparatively small sum, to ensure that they obtain a copy of every single piece of printed matter which is written about you. Similarly, if you are interviewed on radio or television, make sure that someone makes a tape or video. These tapes, together with the press cuttings, can be tremendously helpful when trying to give someone an idea of what your business is all about. You could be in discussion with a new supplier, a new bank, a new partner or member of staff. What people have said about you will give them a rare insight into your business.

So, in your thinking, allow room for PR. Really it is a very necessary prop to your mail order advertising programme. Fortunately, in the United Kingdom, our freedom of the press is probably second to none. This means that a product or service endorsed by the press is instantly a highly acceptable commodity in the eyes of the public.

So make sure your story gets told and make sure that your business lives up to what is written about it.

12. A helping hand

Collaboration amongst like businesses has to be an attractive possibility in any industry, but in mail order it is particularly relevant. The costs of building and maintaining a list are considerable and any shortcut to acquiring new customers has to be intriguing. As we see it, there are five major ways in which mail order companies can collaborate. Here they are.

1. List sales or exchanges
2. Inserts in each other's mailing
3. Joint brochures and leaflets
4. Joint advertising
5. Joint administration/fulfilment

We will look at these various ideas in more detail in a moment, but, first of all, a word about the nature of the company with whom you decide to collaborate. Obviously your products have to be compatible – either because you are dealing with the same sort of people (for instance, you sell children's books, they sell children's toys), or because the products sit harmoniously together (you make garden gnomes, they make garden furniture).

However, doing business with another mail order company is not as simple as that. First, consider the type of market in which you are both involved; by that we mean the social structure of your customers. Are you dealing with the same sort of income group? For example, if you are selling handmade leather-bound children's classic literature, a toy manufacturer selling cheap plastic bits and pieces probably would have a completely different sort of customer from your own. You would do better to deal with somebody who makes, say, handmade wooden toys. We have direct experience of this situation. When we were selling fairly expensive specialist children's clothes, we tried renting a list from a mail order company which concentrated on the sale of a well-known chain store's seconds. It was hopeless – the response was negligible. However, we did team up on a regular basis with a company offering pre-school education and their list worked very well for us.

The second area in which you need to be compatible is even more vital. This is with regard to company policy in the treatment of customers and, indeed, general integrity when it comes to business dealings. Having carefully built and nurtured a reputation for providing a reliable service and a quality product, the whole thing could be blown apart overnight if, for example, you distribute a joint leaflet with a company whose ideas of customer service leave a great deal to be desired. We speak here from bitter experience; quite frankly, we do not think our business ever recovered.

What we would suggest you do before committing yourself to co-operation with another mail order company is to try being their customer. Send off a few orders. When they arrive, send them back asking for a replacement or a refund and see what sort of service you receive. It might prove quite an eye-opener.

Having issued a few stern warnings, let us now look at the advantages of collaboration.

LISTS

Earlier on we came out very strongly against the concept of the list broker – and we stick by that. None the less, mailing to other people's lists and, indeed, hiring out your own can prove very lucrative provided you are careful. Rather than deal through a list broker, we would recommend that you approach direct one or two companies and suggest some form of mutual trading. There are two possible courses of action open to you:

1. You could hire each other's lists, on an exchange basis or for cash.
2. You could buy their list outright.

This is where we would ask you to remember that organisations other than mail order companies have lists. People acquire lists for all sorts of reasons. Companies not involved in mail order often take advertisements inviting customers to send for a brochure and, having enticed their customer into one of their retail stockists, there is no further use for the name. A company might be running a competition, or a promotion, which involves people writing in to them. What about attendances at an exhibition, booking forms from travel agents, theatre reservations, club members? The list is endless, so keep on the look-out for opportunities.

Renting out your own list

There are conflicting schools of thought on this. While some people, and we are amongst them, believe that you should never rent out the names of people who buy from your own brochure on a regular basis, there is a view which suggests that, far from this being a bad thing, it is actually an advantage, since it stimulates people into the habit of buying by mail order. However, the fact is that people only have so much disposable income in any one year and it has to be preferable that they spend it on your brochure rather than someone else's! We

101

would strongly recomend that you do not attempt to rent out your first-class names.

Those people who have sent in one inquiry but have never bought, or who buy very spasmodically, might be well worth renting out. Certainly you can make quite a considerable income from renting out a list, provided you take a few sensible precautions. First, make sure that you and the hirer enter into a form of written agreement, whereby the list will only be used once, except for those customers who order as a result of the mailing. Second, it is important to introduce sleepers – or seeds, as they are sometimes known. This means you place amongst the names you are renting a series of coded names and addresses – for instance, your mother's name at your address, your son's name at your mother's. When the mailing packages come home, you will see what is being sent out to your customer, whether it conforms to the agreement and whether it is used on a one-off basis only. All mail order companies know that this is standard procedure and so very rarely risk abusing the mailing agreement. If you are dealing with a company not in the mail order business, it would be sensible to spell out exactly what you are going to do. This emphasises the point that you may be able to hire out your list not only to mail order companies, but to other sectors of industry, for a one-off purpose – like advertising a new product. Certainly hiring out your list to non-mail order firms greatly reduces the risk of abuse.

In calculating the price you are going to charge for the hiring out of your list, you need to take into account how the buyer wants your names presented. There are four main methods of doing this.

1. Cheshire labels – these labels are specially designed to be applied mechanically, usually by a mailing house. If you do not have a mailing house who can produce Cheshire labels then it is possible that you could provide a computer list, which your customer could then use to produce his or her own Cheshire labels.
2. Self-adhesive labels.
3. Gummed labels.
4. Magnetic tape. This is a new development but it is clearly where the future lies, since it is fast, efficient and cheap.

Your buyer may want the addresses presented in a certain order or in a particular category. For example, the most economical way of mailing large quantities is to use the postal rebate scheme which we discuss in detail in Chapter 14. Many mail order companies store their names in postal rebate regions and your buyer may request this. Alternatively, he or she may request the names in one particular region. In some instances, the buyer may ask for the list to be even more finely tuned, to include a list of customers who have purchased a particular product of yours. We were asked once to hire out a list of people with children under three and, assuming your list is on the computer and that all your orders are fed into it, this degree of detail is quite possible. However, you would not be expected to provide such definition without a considerable increase in fees. Standard list renting fees are around £40–45 per thousand, but they can go way over that for specialist lists.

So there are indeed benefits from renting out your list – all of them financial! Do not allow yourself to become carried away with this though. Take our advice and keep your best customers to yourself.

Renting or buying someone else's list

Always test a list before committing yourself to buying more than 5,000 names and always try to mail new lists with your winning products. It is worth while producing a small catalogue of your winners especially for testing lists, so that you know you are giving a new list the best possible chance. If it does not work for you in ideal circumstances, then you know the lack of response is not in any way connected with the product – the fault must lie with the list.

If you are buying a list, then, as well as testing for response, you also need to go through what is known as the *merge and/or purge* exercise. This means you take the list and compare it with your existing customer list to assess the degree of duplication. If you are renting the list you purge only. If you are buying the list outright, you merge as well! This is a procedure which is virtually always done on computer these days and is comparatively simple, though quite costly. For this reason it would be better if you could specialise on your initial purging exercise. What do we mean by that? Let us assume you are testing 5,000 names and you have an existing customer list of 120,000 names. In order to merge and/or purge successfully, all of the 120,000 names you have will need to be compared with the 5,000 test, and it is on the 120,000 names that the computer time will be calculated and a charge made. If, say, Scotland is a particularly good area for you, it would be sensible to ask for 5,000 Scottish names to test, which could then be compared with the 30,000 Scottish names that you have – thus keeping costs down. The merging and purging of the sample names will tell you whether you need to undertake this exercise on the total list you are intending to use. If the sample duplication factor is high (over 10 per cent), then you should. If less than 10 per cent, it is probably cheaper to mail the duplicated existing customers rather than merge and purge.

It needs to be recognised that if you are collaborating with a like company, the chances are that you will have quite a large duplication of names. Not only are your customers going to be interested in the same type of product, but they are also attracted to buying by mail order. This narrows down the field to the point where there has to be some duplication. In fact if you are given a list by a like company and you find there are little or no duplications with your own active list, then you should be deeply suspicious. You are probably being given names that are ten years out of date!

So now we come to the million dollar question: what should you expect from a successful mailing of someone else's list in terms of response? As a rough guide, we would suggest that 3–4 per cent is very good. However, a great deal depends on the nature of your product and the degree of specialisation you require from the list. If you had demanded, and had allegedly been given, a list of all left-handed mail order buyers in Durham, because you had a product which was aimed at them specifically, then your response should be very high indeed! Again, if you were selling three-piece suites at £900 a time, you might be very happy with a 1 per cent response, or even less. What you must do is to work out the point at which you break even on the cost of acquiring the list and mailing it. If a list does not work at the testing stage, *forget it*, however compatible you feel the products must be. People in the mail order business tend to be tremendous optimists (they have to be!), but if the list is not pulling, regardless of whether you know the reason for it or not, *do not buy it*.

INSERTS IN EACH OTHER'S MAILINGS

Provided you have confidence in the company with whom you are dealing, this is a very good way of acquiring new custom. It is also a good way of earning revenue from your list without the risk of handing over your names to someone else. The normal charge made for inserts is based on the additional cost of postage which will result from including a leaflet in the mailing, plus about £25 per thousand inserts. This, on the face of it, may seem a high fee, but it is quite an inexpensive way of reaching new customers. Remember, the envelope, the handling and the names are included for this charge.

As with mailing to bought-in lists, inserts should be concentrated on displaying your winners. You must judge the value of co-operation with another company in the best possible light. It is certainly not a time to experiment with new products. The chief disadvantage of having your leaflet inserted in someone else's mailing is that you have no way of knowing if it is actually done. After all, in theory your brochure could be dumped in the bin while your so-called collaborating company simply pockets the fee in total. One way round this is to insist on the mailing being done through a reputable mailing house and certainly we would suggest that this is essential if you are looking at a large number of inserts. The only other alternative is to make sure that both you and your friends and staff are on the mailing list of the company with whom you intend doing business, so that you will automatically receive their mailing package. If your leaflet is not enclosed, then you have grounds for complaint.

Inserts should not be large publications in our view – six A5 sheets at the most. If you are accepting someone else's leaflet in your mailing, make sure that in terms of format it is smaller than your own brochure. You do not want it to look as though it is a joint mailing or, worse still, that your brochure is the insert. You must make absolutely sure that your own brochure and inserts dominate the mailing package.

By contrast, of course, the reverse applies if you are inserting in someone else's mailing! Make sure you have sight of their mailing package in advance and concentrate on making your leaflet as dominant as possible, so that it stands out from the rest of the literature. Against this, you need to bear in mind that you will be very lucky if you get more than a 2 per cent response, so you must keep your leaflet production costs as low as possible.

There are dangers, but provided you follow the obvious safeguards you can have excellent results.

JOINT BROCHURES OR LEAFLETS

On the face of it, this is a wonderful idea. You halve everything: the cost of the photography, the cost of printing and the cost of postage. In practice, you must be very careful. Just as you enjoy visiting your local store or supermarket because you know your way around, the same applies to your customer and your brochure. We have stressed the importance of establishing a style and sticking to it, and you are in serious danger of jeopardising that style if you join forces with someone else. What we would recommend is that any joint venture undertaken should be over and above your normal brochure mailing, not instead of it. Think of an excuse for an extra brochure – a summer special, a Christmas extra – some reason for producing a supplement to what you are already doing. Make it quite clear to your customers that this is a one-off and that you have not amalgamated with, or been taken over by, the company whose brochure you are sharing. We cannot stress enough that the public is still deeply suspicious of mail order. If you are seen to have joined forces with another company, particularly a larger one, people may assume you are about to go under.

The other major consideration is that of fulfilment, that is, order processing. You cannot expect a customer to fill in two separate order forms. It is just not practical; it is making everything far too difficult for the customer. So your goods and that of your collaborating mail order company (your 'partner') will need to be ordered on the same order form. On the face of it, you say that may not be a problem. Your partner fulfils his or her part of the order, you fulfil yours. You dispatch them separately and that is the end of the story. Sorry, it is not that simple. Customers will ring up with queries and they need a central number to which to refer. They may be ringing about your product or your partner's, they may want to exchange one of your partner's products for one of your own. The possible ramifications are enough to blow your mind. The only way to cope with the problem is to appoint a fulfilment house to handle centrally all orders. This means that you and your partner each hand over your stock for the fulfilment house to dispatch. If you have your own in-house dispatch department, this may not please you very much, since you will be having to pay extra overheads, but it is the only answer.

You will have to be very careful, too, about the agreement you reach with your partner. However carefully you allocate pages and numbers of products, whatever you call the brochure, or whatever style you use for copy and illustrations, one of you is going to take more money than the other – perhaps considerably more. It will not necessarily be the best-known company, nor the largest of the two, either. However, in these circumstances, whoever has taken the least money will tend to be annoyed about having to pay 50 per cent of the costs. We would suggest that if you feel there may be an imbalance, you should apportion the costs on a pro rata basis, according to response. If you do decide to split the costs fifty–fifty in advance – regardless of who takes what – then make quite sure the agreement is watertight.

JOINT ADVERTISING

All the comments we have made about brochures above apply to advertising, except that in theory you will be advertising fewer products, so rather than use a fulfilment house, it might be possible for one of you to handle all the fulfilment. Again, however, you must be careful to protect your individual image and, whilst occasional joint advertising might prove useful, we would not recommend you to do it on a regular basis since it is bound to cause confusion.

Ideally, when you advertise jointly you should come to an agreement whereby you both retain ownership of all the buyers' names, regardless of which company they bought from. Even given this bonus, we believe joint advertising to be a fairly chancy business. Direct response money-off-the-page advertising is a difficult, unpredictable business. People have tried clubbing together in the past, but, by all accounts, not usually to good effect. Try it once, by all means, but use caution.

JOINT ADMINISTRATION/FULFILMENT

In Chapter 16 we will discuss the pros and cons of having your own despatch department and your own computer against putting out these facilities to specialists. The other alternative is to club together with another mail order company to share the administrative burden. Certainly, as far as computers are concerned, very often in order to acquire a computer with a sufficient number of functions to suit one's requirements it is easy to end up with a great deal of over-capacity. In such a case it is tempting to suggest hiring out that capacity to someone else.

Alternatively, you might find yourself in a position where you can acquire larger premises than you need, which will provide a space for someone to keep their stock – and the natural progression from that is to offer to undertake fulfilment for them.

Beware of all this for two reasons. First, if it is you who is offering the fulfilment facilities, do not forget *what* you are. You are a mail order trader, not a fulfilment house, a warehouse or a computer bureau. By all means offer these extra facilities to colleagues if you feel that such a scheme is compatible with what you are doing. However, *never lose sight of your main objective*. If you do, you may find yourself in a position where your warehouse is full of other people's stock, just when you need it for yourself.

Second, if you are using someone else's facilities, you must recognise that you will tend to lose the personal feel, as far as your business is concerned. We had a period when our orders were sent to another mail order company who processed and dispatched for us. It was a disaster. All the statistics in the world cannot compensate for being able to see and touch what is going on. Once the sacks of mail stopped coming through our door, we found it increasingly difficult to gauge response on a day-to-day basis. Certainly we received the computer print-outs, but somehow it was not nearly as satisfactory and, far more important, our customer service completely lost its personal touch. Of course, this may not be relevant if you are a large concern, but for small businesses we would suggest you should be very careful about handing over too many vital areas of administration to another mail order concern. Do not risk losing the feel of your own business.

Collaboration with other mail order companies has to be a good thing – in moderation. However, beware – it is easy to become carried away and find yourself too firmly enmeshed in a relationship before you have had a chance to consider the implications. Yet properly handled, with a degree of reserve, we would suggest that the rest of the mail order industry has a lot to offer you.

13. Mail order overseas

This is not an area into which you should enter lightly. However, the fact is that if you have a good idea which is selling well in the UK, chances are it will sell in a number of other places in the world as well. This really is the crux of the matter. Do not even consider mail order outside the UK until you have established a good solid base in this country. It is hopeless to use overseas mail order as an excuse. By that we mean that if you find business here not as brisk as you would like, you might be tempted to look for fresh markets. *This has to be wrong*. Learn the ropes here and get to understand the business from top to bottom. In the UK you start with a basis of knowing a lot about your home market; if you cannot attract sales here, there is either something wrong with you, your business or you product. Sorry to be so brutal, but that has to be the fact.

If you do have a solid sales base in the UK, however, the attractions of looking overseas are considerable. Such is the balance of our economy that markets here dry up from time to time, or become unstable, and quite apart from any other consideration a market outside the country does provide a degree of insurance. Undoubtedly mail order overseas is most successful, and most often used, in approaching foreign industry rather than the individual consumer. However, there are a number of businesses selling consumer goods overseas very successfully. It is all a question, as with everything, of establishing a market.

Establishing an export market for your product requires you to undertake much the same work as we have outlined in the first section of this book, except that you will be aiming your researches at the particular country or countries of your choice. Obtain a copy of every relevant publication you can, visit the country and talk to people who understand the market. If as a result of these inquiries you feel there really is a market for your product, then there are two things you must acquire – a good advertising agency in the country of your choice and a secretary or member of staff within your own organisation who speaks the language fluently.

We would not recommend that you attempt direct response advertising, at least not until you have a very well-established toe-hold in the country. Direct mail is likely to generate the best results. How you acquire your mailing list will depend considerably on your type of business. Certainly if you are mailing to potential industrial and commercial customers, this should not prove too difficult, since names can be supplied by the relevant trade associations. The consumer is a different matter, however. If you believe you can make an approach direct to a foreign consumer, we would recommend that the product you select is of a very specialist nature, thus making it easier to define your market.

As part of your decision-making process, you should contact the Post Office who have some very helpful literature on the subject of export. You should also seek the advice of a local freight forwarder, so that you appreciate the implications of duty and VAT, all of which can be prohibitive in cost or administrative terms to your whole enterprise.

You can look on direct mail abroad in two ways. Either the whole operation can be conducted from the UK, or you could set up a satellite distribution point in your chosen country. On the whole, we would recommend the former, at least until you have established a market. Quite apart from the costs of setting up a separate unit, there is also the problem of staffing it properly and keeping control. In some countries, where there is an exchange control problem, this may not be possible and you may be forced to operate from within the country. If you can establish a direct relationship with your customer, the Post Office have made a couple of suggestions which we think are very useful.

1. Rather than use a franking machine to stamp your envelope when mailing abroad, use traditional stamps instead. The sight of UK stamps, particularly the larger attractive ones, will ensure that your mail order literature is opened.
2. Always include reply paid envelopes. Customers do not want to feel at a disadvantage in buying from a foreign country. If they

have to pay a high rate of postage in order to place an order, they will feel they are behaving irresponsibly.

Whilst it is very important to understand the psyche of the people to whom you are mailing, do not be afraid of your product or service appearing too British. After all, this is what you are selling – a British product – and what you have to do is to convince your would-be customer that there is something special about it. One of its most special attractions has to be that it is foreign. Whilst it is necessary for the main literature to be in the language of the country to whom you are selling, a spattering of English around a brochure will not matter. Similarly, as far as labelling is concerned, providing that labels conform to the country's legal requirements with regard to material composition, etc., actually having an English label, as opposed to a French, German or Spanish one, is probably a good idea. It could also be cost effective too, since presumably the label will be in production already.

On the subject of advertising literature, do not try to be too inventive. If you have found a formula of presentation which works in the UK, it will probably work everywhere else, too. You are testing one completely new element – your market – so try to make as many of the other aspects in the presentation the same as your most successful campaign to date. You do not want to find yourself in the position where you are saying, 'Is it that the French market does not like us, or is it that the brochure is at fault, or is it that we should have left our product red instead of changing it to green?' As with list testing, concentrate on exploiting *known successes*. If they do not work, then probably you are in the wrong market.

This attitude will also help keep costs down. It may even be possible to use your existing brochure, particularly if you have followed our advice and kept the copy black, in which case it is a question of re-making the black plate in the appropriate language. Alternatively, you could consider a shell folder. You can print a fantastic four-colour folder, showing the range of your products and quoting your company name and logo, which will apply for any country in the world. Then, inside the folder, you can print off details in whatever language is appropriate. Whatever literature you adopt, try not to compromise your existing style too much in order to accommodate overseas mailing.

In conclusion, if you feel your product may have overseas appeal, make sure you do your research properly and gather around you expert help. It could provide an exciting new dimension to your business.

PART 3. THE MECHANICS

We have discussed the concept of your selling by mail order and also how to set about marketing your wares. What we have not discussed are the implications of doing so.

Many people labour under the misapprehension that selling by mail order is an easy way of going into business. After all, it is surely just a question of producing a catalogue, or taking space in a newspaper, and then waiting for the orders to flow. What they tend to totally overlook is the servicing aspect of running a mail order business, which is far from simple.

Selling by mail order is a considerable administrative headache – a far bigger one than can be possibly envisaged without having had personal experience. You need a business structure, systems, finance and the right people helping you – but, above all, you need the right attitude.

We hope the remaining chapters of this book will provide a foundation from which you can establish a basic business structure which in turn will support your marketing plans.

14. Distribution: the Post Office and its competitors

Distribution is a fundamental part of every mail order business and for this reason we decided it was the best place to start when looking at the mechanics of mail order. Distribution falls into two categories:

1. the mailing of your promotional material;
2. the dispatch of goods.

In this chapter we will be looking at the relative services being offered by the Post Office and by individual carriers. Next to advertising, distribution is going to be your biggest item of expenditure and it is vital therefore to ensure that not only is it efficient, but also as inexpensive as possible.

POST OFFICE SERVICES

While still in the early planning stages of your business – long before you start work on your brochure, or buy, or manufacture, your goods – you need to sit down and have a good long discussion with your local

Post Office representative. The deals he or she can offer you, the schemes that are available and the discounted rates of postage which apply to mail order are a fundamental part of your business plan. In fact the implications of distribution are more far-reaching than any plan. They go right to the very heart of your business – to the product itself. If you are designing, for example, a portable television to sell by mail order, a major factor in its technical development might be that, packaged and ready to dispatch, it weighs no more than 25 kilograms – hence falling within the Post Office delivery bracket for weight. This fact alone could determine whether or not the whole scheme is a marketable proposition.

How you dispatch your goods and what they are going to cost you is bound to affect all of your forecasting. Similarly, all of your plans will depend upon the size of your direct mailings. Whether you can afford to mail 10,000 or 100,000 leaflets is going to make a vast difference to your sales projections. So do appreciate the importance of distribution in your overall business planning and make it one of your first priorities to decide how your mailings will be sent out and your goods dispatched.

Let us look in more detail at what facilities the Post Office have to offer.

Direct mailing services

There are nine distinct Post Office services which are particularly relevant to the mail order industry:

> First- and second-class letter contracts
> Electronic post
> Overseas direct mail
> Business reply
> Freepost
> Private boxes
> Household delivery
> First-day cover service
> Admail

Let us look at each of these services in more detail.

First- and second-class letter contracts If you can pre-sort your letter mailings into postal regions and you are mailing more than 5,000 envelopes, you qualify for a discount, provided your mailing is to domestic addresses, rather than industrial ones. The discount rates vary according to whether your envelopes are postcoded and whether you are sending your letters by first- or second-class mail. However, as a guide, you can expect between 10 and 14 per cent discount. As an alternative, if you are prepared to accept delivery within seven working days, you can qualify for a considerable reduction in rate on that of the normal second-class mail – the Post Office quote up to 30 per cent as being possible. This particular discount is known as bulk rebate and applies on all mailing of over 4,250 items – again sorted into postal regions.

The implications of these facilities are enormous when it comes to looking at your overall postage charges. Certainly, when setting up your mailing lists you should have them stored in Post Office rebate regions, and when renting or buying in someone else's list the price you pay will be substantially dictated according to whether the list is rebate sorted or not. It would be sensible here to describe the term *rebate*. To qualify for discount, you need to negotiate a contract with the Post Office. When it comes to paying for your postage, you are expected to pay the full rate and then the Post Office rebate the appropriate discount to you. This is not as onerous as it seems, since the Post Office will give you credit terms if you are a reputable company, so that hopefully you will be reaping the benefit of your mailing in terms of cash sales before you actually have to pay for the postage. However, for purposes of cash-flow, you do need to recognise that initially you will be paying the *full postage rate* prior to receiving your rebate.

Another facility available is printed postage impressions. (PPI). PPI is an alternative to stamps or franking machines. On application to the Post Office, you are given a PPI number, as a result of which you can have all your mailing envelopes pre-printed with your own code which clearly saves an enormous amount of time. However, you cannot use PPI envelopes for posting any letter, as you can with a franking machine. It depends on a minimum letter mailing of 5,000.

New mail order companies qualify for a free mailing if they mail two thousand items or more. There is a sliding scale: The more you mail, the greater the number of free items you can send. Details are given below.

Size of first-time mailing	Free postage element	
	1st class	2nd class
No. of items	items	items
Up to 1,999	1,000	1,300
2,000–2,999	1,250	1,500
3,000–3,999	1,500	1,800
4,000–7,499	2,000	2,400
7,500–9,999	2,250	2,700
Over 10,000	2,500	3,000

All the rebate schemes and special rates we have mentioned apply to items which weigh no more than 60 grams. This is quite a generous allowance. You can dispatch a fairly hefty catalogue, including a letter, inserts and a reply paid envelope, within this weight limit. However, it is vital that you weigh your mailing very carefully before committing yourself to such things as the number of inserts you are including, the quality of your paper, etc. The Post Office say that all too frequently mailing houses do not take advantage of the 60-gram limit – in other words, their mailings are very light and they could mail far more for the money they are paying. It is an interesting concept, suggesting that since you are spending so much on the envelope, the stuffing and the postage, you might as well get your money's worth! You could achieve this either by offering more items for sale, or perhaps by earning extra revenue from inserting someone else's leaflet in your mailing package.

Finally, it should be noted that the Post Office are surprisingly flexible and very anxious to help mail order businesses. Certainly, if you are a bulk user of their facilities, sending out large mailings several times a year, they will not penalise you if a mailing does not quite reach the minimum requirement in terms of numbers.

Electronic post You provide the Post Office with magnetic tape of names and addresses, plus the text of a letter. They will then print the letter, together with your company name, logo and signature, place each letter in an envelope, and mail it to reach your customers the following day. Prices vary, of course, according to the format of your letter and the size of the mailing, but 20p per letter would seem to be a fairly average price. When one considers this includes paper, printing, envelope, inserting the letter in the envelope and postage, it really is an amazing service – not to mention, speedy. The snags are that at present the letter can only be printed in black and white and also your tape must be compatible with the Post Office computer.

Overseas direct mail The Post Office are very keen to encourage direct mail export and to this end they are prepared to make a contribution to your first export mailing. This contribution, like the inland first-time mailing, is on a sliding scale, as shown in the table.

Total postage cost of first-time mailing £	Free postage contribution £
Up to 399	200
400–599	250
600–799	300
800–1,499	400
1,500–1,999	500
2,000 and over	550

You are eligible for the postage contribution whether you are going into mail order for the first time, or simply making your first overseas direct mail shot.

Business reply As we have already discussed, your response rate will be greatly enhanced it you can make it as easy as possible for the customer to respond. To this end, the business reply envelope, or label, is an obvious choice. The Post Office understand your need to test before adopting such a scheme, and so they offer a free trial. If you

116

wish to try out the scheme, they will waive your first annual licence fee – which normally costs £20 – and also pay postage and handling charges on your first 300 replies, provided they are under 60 grams and are received within the first free licence year.

You can choose whether you wish the reply service to come to you first or second class, and the costs are the normal postage rate, plus 5p on every reply you receive. Bearing in mind that you still have to pay for the cost of the envelope, this is not a particularly cheap facility, though you may well find the difference it makes to your response rate worth the additional cost involved.

Freepost   If your business is granted a Freepost licence, you simply put the words *FREEPOST (no stamp required)* in your address line on all your direct response advertising. This means that your customers do not need to pay postage on their replies. The Post Office charges for Freepost are exactly the same as for business reply – the difference being that the customer has to provide the envelope, which cuts costs from your point of view. As with business reply, you can have a trial run with Freepost, on the same basis, to see if it works for you.

Private boxes   With the death of a second postal delivery in the day (except during the Christmas period), you could find that the normal once-a-day service is not frequent enough for your business, particularly if you are receiving replies from a very successful mail shot. One enormous batch of mail each day could disrupt your general administration and order processing. To resolve that problem, the Post Office can provide you with a private box and you can collect your mail from it at anytime during the day, rather than wait for normal deliveries.

Household delivery   Because thousands of postmen are delivering to millions of homes every day, the Post Office have introduced a door-to-door distribution service for unaddressed mail. In other words, if you have some promotional material which you would like delivered into a number of homes, these can be included on the postman's normal round and he will push them through letterboxes with the mail. You can choose the area of the country in which you wish this to be done, and the rates are quite reasonable, as listed in the table.

	Items up to 35 grams £ per 1,000	Items over 35 grams and up to 60 grams £ per 1,000
Distribution		
Up to 10,000	36.00	40.00
10,001–20,000	33.00	37.00
20,001–50,000	29.50	34.00
50,001–100,000	26.50	31.50
100,001–500,000	23.00	28.50
500,001–10,000,000	20.50	27.50
In excess of 1,000,000	19.50	27.00

Of course, it needs to be recognised that a leaflet which has not been personally addressed is not going to encourage the same response as if it was sent through the post in the normal way. However, we believe that the Post Office do score with this service over other leaflet distributors. Because the leaflet is delivered with the normal day's post, it carries more authority. Not only that, in our view, it is far less likely to end up in the bin, without even being looked at. The arrival of the post in people's homes is an event. Care is taken to sift it into piles for each member of the household. If your leaflet is included in this ritual, the chances are it will at least be looked at, even if ultimately discarded. A leaflet stuffed through your letterbox at random, if not eaten by the dog, will probably be trampled underfoot long before anybody even notices it is there. We should just mention that for this Post Office service there is a minimum charge of £100 per distribution.

First-day cover service Using the first-day cover service is a good way of making your advertising stand out from the rest of the mail. The Post Office have a number of their own designs for printing on to envelopes, or you can design your own. These are in full colour and are usually combined with a special postmark on the first day of a new stamp issue. The service is far from cheap, but it does make the envelope look very special indeed. We would suggest you ask your postal representative for details of this service, as prices do vary enormously, according to what sort of design you require.

Admail This is a very useful marketing device for mail order companies. Suppose you were making and supplying Brighton rock, but happened to live in Burton-on-Trent. Naturally you would be on the horns of a dilemma, since you would want your address to be seen as Brighton. Suppose you were selling Scottish kilts, but your works were in Falmouth, you would prefer your address to read, say, Edinburgh. Under the Post Office's Admail scheme this is quite possible. You are allocated a PO box number; you give the main town address of you choice, but your post goes nowhere near it – the PO box number is simply a code as far as the Post Office is concerned. The Admail facility can be used in conjunction with Freepost or Business Reply and is a very useful marketing device. Again, you should ask your postal representative for a quotation.

These then are the main direct mail services offered by the Post Office. As you will see, the various options are considerable and really, considering the degree of service, very economic. Now let us look at the distribution of goods.

Distribution of goods

There are two sorts of parcel: the letter packet and the parcel. Letter packets start at a weight of 60 grams and go on up to a kilogram. Parcels start at half a kilogram and go up to 25 kilograms. As you will

118

see, there is a degree of overlap between the letter packet and the parcel; where this occurs you can select which of the two methods you wish to use. The advantage of the letter packet is that it can be sent first class or second class. First-class letter packets are more expensive than parcels, but only marginally so. Second-class letter packets are actually cheaper than parcels of the same weight. The best plan is to juggle between the three rates, using the best of all of them where you can.

Just as with direct mailing, the Post Office has looked at ways of saving their customers' time and money. These are the facilities available:

> Contract service
> Rebates
> Cash on delivery
> Signature on delivery
> Returnable parcels
> Insurance
> Zonal distribution
> Bookpost
> Datapost
> Overseas mailing

Let us look at these in more detail.

Contract service This is the most important service as far as the dispatch of goods is concerned. If you sign a contract with the Post Office you no longer have to weigh and stamp each parcel and a van will come and collect your parcels from your warehouse at regular intervals (often several times a day if you have sufficient volume). The contract works by the use of various PPI labels, printed to show whether you are sending parcels or first- or second-class letter packets. These labels are attached to your parcels and then, rather than weigh each parcel individually, you are charged on the average weight per consignment. This saves an inordinate amount of time both for you and the Post Office. There are special trial offers to be had to enable you to test various weights and you should talk to your postal sales representative about this.

Rebates If you dispatch more than 4,250 identical packets, you are eligible for a substantial rebate. It is not possible to quote rates here, as they will vary according to circumstances. Again, though, you can obtain a quotation.

Cash on delivery For payment of a fee in addition to normal postage, the Post Office will deliver your parcel or packet and collect payment from the addressee. The cash is paid to you within five working days of delivery and each day's total will reach you in the form of a single Giro cheque. This is obviously a very useful service and it is far cheaper than invoicing, since chasing money is a very costly process.

Signature on delivery This is a receipted parcel service, where the addressee is asked to sign the postman's receipt book which provides a record of delivery should you ever require it. Each parcel is given a numbered label which is supplied by the Post Office. This service is most useful, obviously, where valuable goods are involved.

Returnable parcels If you are offering goods on approval, you should recognise that it is preferable to make the return of goods as easy as possible. This being the case, you can offer your customer the facility of having the parcel paid for if they wish to send back the goods. This creates a great deal of confidence and, of course, need not be restricted to goods on approval – it is a facility which you could offer at the point of purchase. It is costly, however, and not widely used.

Insurance Under the Post Office code of practice, they will pay compensation for any parcel lost, up to a value of £17. However, they also run a scheme called the Compensation Fee Parcel Service. By contributing to this scheme you can claim compensation up to the replacement value of the goods. It is well worth investigating.

Zonal distribution You can enjoy a considerably reduce postage rate for parcels posted and delivered within specified area – either in a group of counties, or perhaps a large city. It is difficult to envisage this situation arising where a national mail order company is concerned, but it is possible that you might have run a competition or advertised in a specific area which has excited purely local response. Next day delivery is guaranteed and there are not the same restrictions on size and weight as with normal parcels, nor is the same degree of pro-tectived packaging required as with normal post. Certainly, if you see yourself mailing in a specific area, it is worth looking at this service.

Bookpost A special service has been set up to assist the distribution of books. The Post Office, working closely with the Book Publishers' Association, have introduced specific facilities to help publishers and book traders generally. If you are distributing over 10,000 parcels per annum, there are very big discounts to be enjoyed, but even for less than this amount, there are discounts of up to 15 per cent available without the need for any pre-sorting. If you are in the bookselling business, this is well worth investigating.

Datapost Datapost guarantee a next day delivery of goods up to 27.5 kilograms to any point in Britain. It is not a cheap service, but it is fast and compares very favourably with independent express services. In the normal course of events, it is not something you would use in a mail order business, but now and again it could act as a wonderful panacea for a disgruntled customer!

Mail order overseas Datapost also offer an international service, quoting amazing times – like London to Bahrain in 24 hours, Aberdeen to Zurich in 48 hours, Birmingham to Tokyo in 72 hours, and Manchester to the Hague in 24 hours. If your order value is high enough, this could well be worth while. Some of your goods may even travel by Concorde!

Frankly, given this range of services, in our view it is practically impossible to better the Post Office. Certainly, as far as direct mailing is concerned, there is nothing to touch them, so all you have to consider is whether you would be better advised to distribute your goods by some other means of transport.

DISTRIBUTORS OTHER THAN THE POST OFFICE

There are national carriers who can compete with the Post Office in offering a parcel service which delivers anywhere in the UK. There are also national carriers who specialise in handling the storage and distribution of bulkier/heavier goods; this really is the main area for serious consideration. In our view it is only when you have a specialist requirement such as this that you need look further afield. Carriers competing with the Post Office on normal parcel deliveries find it hard to match Post Office rates, although their service may justify higher prices.

A word of warning – do not use a little transport firm round the corner from your works, however insistent they may be that they can arrange national distribution. They will either be pricey or inefficient, or more likely both. If you are looking for national transport other than the Post Office, go to the big boys. Another point is that even some of the bigger haulage firms are not really able to offer a comprehensive mail order service. Many of them are geared purely to distribution on a business-to-business basis. It is quite another thing delivering to the individual consumer, and you need to be sure they really can cope.

There are four major companies who we consider it worth while to mention here, since they may be able to offer you something which the Post Office cannot. Addresses are supplied at the end of the book.

Lex Wilkinson Ltd

Lex Wilkinson offer their *Homeline* parcel delivery service, under a standard published tariff. Their charge consists of a fixed amount per parcel, plus an additional carriage charge per kilogram. They offer the alternatives of standard delivery or, for a slightly increased cost, delivery against signature from the recipient to establish proof of delivery. They say that the majority of deliveries are made within five working days of collection, with a national average of four days.

Distribution Services Ltd

Distribution Services offer a national storage and delivery facility for bulkier and heavier items, such as three-piece suites or other large furniture. There is no published tariff, because costs will depend very largely on individual customers' precise requirements and, of course, their volume.

Securicor Ltd

Securicor is no stranger to our high streets. They are best known for handling pay rolls and generally the shipment of money and valuables from one place to another. They do, however, offer next day delivery for items required in a hurry. They represent the alternative to Datapost and, of course, are able to take much heavier and bulkier items.

Tibbett and Britten Ltd

Tibbett and Britten are the major distributors of hanging garments. Without a doubt, if you are selling suits, jackets or overcoats, even the best parcel in the world will have them arriving at your customer looking crumpled. Since these items will have been expensive to purchase, presentation is very important and hanging garments, when delivered, do look very good. Prices are subject to negotiation. It is impossible in the case of Tibbett and Britten to make any direct comparison with ordinary mailing costs, but for quality items we would consider it well worth while building distribution in this way into your costings. It will reduce returns drastically.

In trying to establish the best way of handling your distribution, do remember that delivery costs are a major factor as far as mail order transactions are concerned. Also remember that between 10 and 25 per cent of goods will be returned. If, as in the case of heavy furniture, part of your sales promotion is the offer of free transport on any goods returned, you could be looking at a very costly exercise indeed. One distribution company we talked to said that 25 per cent of their customers' transport costs were caused by returns.

If you do decide to deal with an independent carrier, make sure you negotiate a contract. Do not rely on a casual relationship. Let's face it, the standard and efficiency of your delivery service can be the difference between make and break as far as your mail order business is concerned.

Only use a carrier with a fully computerised system, so that every package can be located at any time within the delivery network. Inevitably you are going to receive inquiries from customers and you must be able to tell them when they can expect their goods.

Of course you may be forced to operate outside the Post Office network simply by the nature of the goods you are selling. If you have a choice, however, we do not consider there is really a decision to be made. We have one of the best postal systems in the world, despite all the flak we give it, and in recent years the Post Office has gone out of its way to try and help mail order businesses – well aware of how important they are to its overall growth.

Let us use a brief personal case history to demonstrate one of the many advantages of the Post Office. Because we both work, we are often not at home and while we are away the house is looked after by Mrs Scott, who lives a few doors up the road. When a parcel arrives for us, Colin, the postman, first tries our door. If it is locked and there is no reply, he delivers the parcel instead to Mrs Scott. This is not an arrangement that we have especially set up; it has simply emerged. We live in a small community where everyone knows everyone else and so the postman is an integral part or that community.

The point is that this arrangement is absolutely typical of hundreds and thousands up and down the country. With the best will in the world, no independent delivery network can compete on this level. They just do not have the coverage or the familiarity with the neighbourhood scene. As a mail order company you want your goods delivered fast, efficiently, cheaply and *personally*. Wherever possible, tailormake your merchandise to suit our national postal system.

15. Setting up your business

In previous chapters we have dealt quite specifically with the various aspects of trading by mail order, but there are certain basic rules of business structure which need to be applied whatever your industry. Some of you of course will already have an existing operation which you are intending to expand into mail order, in which case much of this chapter will not apply to you. However, if you are setting up from scratch, let us look at the main factors which you will need to consider before you are in a position to go into business.

TRADING STRUCTURE

Like any business people, mail order traders have a choice as to how they operate their business; to a large extent, the structure they choose will depend upon size of business operation. The first golden rule in the establishment of any business is to recognise that all your business affairs must be kept entirely separate from your personal dealings. You must have a separate bank account and a separate accounting system. This rule is fundamental to every type of business, big or small, and with this firmly in mind let us look at the three main methods of trading.

The sole trader

This is the simplest and therefore the most common form of trading. Provided you have a product or service to sell and sufficient funds to provide it, in theory you can start trading tomorrow. One is inclined to think of sole traders as one-person businesses, but as a sole trader you can employ as many people as you like and there is no restriction at all as to the size of your operation. In fact there are a number of very large concerns in this country which trade in this way.

To operate as a sole trader, there are only three legal requirements:

1. You must keep an up-to-date set of books and records for tax purposes. The tax authorities have the right to inspect these and may do so from time to time, though such records are vital to the successful running of your business in any case. If you are intending to apply to one of the MOP schemes for the right to place money-off-the-page advertisements, you will be expected to produce at least your most recent set of accounts.

2. If your sales are over a certain limit, you will have to register for VAT. Once you have decided on a promotion budget for your first year of trading, you will have some idea as to your projected turnover. If it is likely to exceed the current VAT limit, you should register before you start trading. It is important to contact your local VAT office as soon as possible. You will find them very helpful and they will be able to advise you as to what rules apply to your particular business.

3. If you are intending to employ anyone, you will have to comply with a wide range of legislation. You need to familiarise yourself with the rules relating to hiring, firing, sick pay, maternity leave, sex discrimination and the Race Relations Act. You will also need to make PAYE returns.

   In these circumstances, it is best to go along and see your local DHSS and tax office who will provide you with all the paperwork you need and will explain to you exactly what is required. Again, rather like the VAT office, they have a reputation for being tyrants, but in fact most small businesses find them very helpful.

There are a number of advantages in being a sole trader. Above all, it is simple. The sole trader has no shareholders or co-directors to whom he or she is answerable. Unlike a limited company, there is no requirement to register your accounts for all the world to see. In a nation somewhat beleaguered by red tape, the sole trader will attract the very minimum. Clearly you are attracted by the idea of running your own business or you would not be reading this book. As a sole trader, you most certainly do have your *own* business.

The disadvantages, however, cannot be ignored. As a sole trader, you are 100 per cent responsible for any debts you incur, unlike a limited partnership or company. If your business is in trouble and faces bankruptcy, unsatisfied creditors can pursue you, not only for the assets of the business, but also for your personal assets as well. For this reason, before embarking on business as a sole trader, it might be sensible to transfer your major assets, such as your house, into your spouse's name, so that in the event of failure at least your home is protected.

This advice is not intended to encourage you to have a cavalier attitude towards your debts, but in our view any business venture you undertake should not jeopardise the family home, particularly where children are involved.

The other main disadvantage of being a sole trader is that it is often difficult to be recognised as a business entity in your own right. On the whole, banks prefer lending money to limited companies; landlords prefer granting leases to companies; and private investors are more attracted to investing in a company. The inference is that as a sole trader, although you may have built up a sizeable business, the business remains dependent upon you. If something happens to you, then there is no business left. There may be no justification for this attitude, but it is a view which is prevalent and worthy of consideration.

Partnerships

There are a number of reasons why you might want a partner. It could be that the business requires two people to operate it. It could be that you want moral support, or perhaps you need some financial help. Many business partnerships are a husband and wife team and this can work very well indeed (we should know!).

If, for whatever reason, you need a partner but you are not married to a suitable candidate, then you should be particularly careful! As a general rule we do not favour going into business with friends. The ideal relationship is one where two people get together to form a business because, commercially, it makes sense for them to do so. Having established the business, if the partnership is successful, a friendship will follow. Going into partnership with somebody simply because you enjoy meeting them for a pint once a week is the worst possible motive for choosing a partner. You need to join forces with someone whose skills complement your own, giving as wide a range of abilities between you as possible. You need a balanced relationship. In other words, what you put into the business should be directly related to what you take out. You do not have to be equal partners, as long as the relationship between work and rewards is accurately calculated.

Whatever the relationship between you and your potential partner, you need a written partnership agreement – even if your partner is your husband or wife. 'Surely that's not necessary,' you declare. 'I implicitly trust my husband/wife.' We do not wish to sound unnecessarily pessimistic, but marriages, just like business partnerships, all too often fail and, grim though it sounds, you should make provision for that possibility. You both need protection.

Any solicitor can help you draw up a standard partnership agreement, though probably it will need to be adapted to suit your own particular case. What you should bear in mind is that your partnership agreement will sit in the filing cabinet collecting dust for ever *unless something goes wrong* – with your business, or with your relationship.

This is what you and your partner need to ask one another: 'What happens if the business gets into terrible debt; if one of us is chronically ill or dies; if the premises are burnt down; if we start to hate the sight of each other?' You must consider every eventuality and make sure that if there is a split in the partnership, all partners will be fairly treated.

In a partnership, both partners normally share the profits on a fifty–fifty basis and, accordingly, are jointly responsible for the liabilities of the business. However, you can create a limited partnership. In this event, one or more of the partners can opt for a *limited liability*. This means that in the event of things going wrong, the partner with limited liability is only liable to meet creditors' claims up to the amount he or she has invested in the partnership. In other words, if the business fails with your firm owing Mr Brown £10,000, if your limited liability is £2,000, it would be up to your partner to find the rest. It should be understood that in every partnership one partner must be prepared to accept unlimited liability. Limited partnerships must be registered with the Registrar of Companies and there is a small amount of stamp duty payable on their formation.

The main disadvantage of a partnership is that the success of the business is largely dependent on the relationship you have with your partner. People and circumstances change. When times are difficult, even the best relationships can go sour.

Remember, too, that you are responsible for each other's actions. Whilst the bank account can be controlled by you and your partner being joint signatories on all cheques, there is nothing to stop one partner ordering, for example, £25,000 worth of good on behalf of the partnership. Failure to pay for these goods would be your joint responsibility.

It should be remembered that partnerships are not restricted to two people. You can form a partnership with three or more, though one is tempted to say that the more partners you have, the greater your potential problems!

The limited company

A completely separate legal entity is created by the formation of a limited company. Company law is very complicated, but the setting up of small private company can be quickly and simply done for a comparatively small cost. You can approach the Registrar of Companies yourself, complete the necessary documentation, and form a company without any legal advice. However, we would strongly recommend that you employ the services of a solicitor to ensure that the company is properly set up. He or she will probably recommend that you buy an established company off the shelf, which is the cheapest and quickest method. To form a company, you need a minimum of two directors, one of whom will also need to be company secretary, unless – as in many cases – your solicitor volunteers for that appointment. There are considerable advantages in your solicitor acting as company secretary, as there is a degree of paperwork associated with the job – such as drawing up the minutes and filing the annual returns. However, it should be remembered that your solicitor will not be doing it for love!

One of the problems people normally associate with buying a company off the shelf is the name. The registration agent gives each company a working name and some of them are extremely odd. However, the name of your company need not be the name under which you trade, although do make sure your company name appears on all your promotional material – this is a legal requirement. If you do not want the complication of having your trading name different from your company name, you can file a new company name with the Registrar, provided it is not already in use.

One obligation imposed upon a limited company, which does not apply to the sole trader or partnership, is that annual accounts have to be prepared for the Registrar of Companies. This is not a particular disadvantage in our view, since quite clearly up-to-date records are a requirement of any successful business. The preparation of accounts will require an audit by firm of acountants and, undoubtedly, the cost of the annual audit fee is yet another factor which needs to be taken into account when making a decision as to how you are going to trade.

Having outlined the various trading options, we strongly recommend that you opt for a limited company when trading by mail order. One has to accept that mail order is a somewhat speculative business. If you do your homework correctly, if you start from a strong capital base and – let's face it – if you are lucky, you will succeed. None the less, there are plenty of good business ideas that have sunk without trace and yours could just be one of them.

The kind of business venture that is set up on the promise of a large contract, or a business which requires little investment but your time, is far less likely to fail than a mail order business. By the time you have invested in an advertising programme and stock, inevitably you will have a fairly large commitment on your hands and you need to recognise that unless you are protected by a limited company any debts incurred if things go wrong will be yours, personally.

FINANCIAL PLANNING

Business structure is not simply about how you intend to trade. Let's face it, being in business, especially in the early stages, is all about money and having enough of it. It should be recognised that borrowing money to set up a mail order business is not easy, unless you are backed by some other activity – such as being a manufacturer. Let us consider the start-up costs. The two most obvious requirements are capital for promotional expenditure and for stock. However, depending on what that stock is, you may well require premises and either in-house or external computer systems for list maintenance, stock control, customer services, etc. The three most important figures in your life are *sales, gross profit* and *overheads* – the largest overhead by far being your cost of promotion. These three figures, and the relationship between them, are all important to your success or failure. A high gross profit (gross profit being the difference between your sales and your cost of a sales, that is, your manufacturing costs or your buying costs) could justify a high promotional spend. On the other hand, if your gross profit is liable to be low, you must keep your advertising costs very much under control.

Before you can begin to commit yourself to either an advertising spend or a large purchase of stock, you must first work out a *profit plan*. Both words are important. *Profit* is the reason you are in business. *Plan* means just that – not an optimistic target, not the minimum achievable if virtually everything goes wrong, not a set of figures pulled out of the air, nor indeed what you think your bank manager wants to

hear. A *profit plan* represents your careful assessment of what you reasonably believe you will achieve, setting natural caution against natural optimism. We set out below the steps you need to take in the preparation of your plan.

The second stage of the operation is to produce a *cash forecast*. Here again, we will take you step by step through the exercise. Having satisfied yourself via the profit plan that the business is viable, you must then use the same figures to plot cash in and cash out on a monthly basis. This will then give you your working capital requirement.

The profit plan

1. Prepare yourself a chart with twelve monthly columns for your first year of trading, starting with the month in which you will open the doors for the first time, plus an additional column for the annual total. Ideally, with a new business, you should be looking at your first two years of operation, but this is somewhat difficult with a mail order business, as it is difficult to project ahead without any track record of achievement.

2. The first figure you put down is sales, on a month-by-month basis, remembering to reflect the gradual build-up of trade which you may be expecting and seasonal trends where they apply. The sales figures should be shown net of VAT. We appreciate it is very difficult to gauge this figure without experience, but seek help and advice. You must be confident about a minimum sales figure to go into business at all.

3. You should then calculate your direct costs on those sales, again net of VAT. If you are manufacturing a product, your direct costs will be raw materials, components and productive labour. If you are merely buying and selling a product, your direct costs will be your purchase price. The difference between your sales figure and your direct costs is the *gross profit*.
4. The gross profit is a very important benchmark in the mail order business. Of course the gross profit margin may vary somewhat from product to product, but you should typically be looking for a figure of around 65 per cent in order to cover your costs. Needless to say, in order to sleep at night your gross profit must exceed your total overheads!
5. This brings us to the overheads. There are several pointers you need to watch for in calculating your overheads on a month-by-month basis. First of all, do make sure you include *everything*. It is too easy to miss out items, only to get a nasty shock later on. The other point to bear in mind is that your overheads should be recorded, not as they fall due for payment, but spread over the period in which they are relevant. In other words, to take a simple example, your rent may be paid quarterly, but you should show the rent allocation monthly, so that the profit calculation for each month can be assessed with its full share of overheads.

By contrast, some overheads may be affected by the amount of sales you generate. An obvious example of this is postage – the higher your sales, the higher your postage costs will be.

It might be useful here just to clarify the differences between direct and indirect labour costs. As already mentioned above, that element of your labour costs which is directly involved in the manufacturing process should be shown as cost of sales – hence the term *direct labour*. Those members of your staff who are involved in general duties – your accountant, secretaries, order processors, warehouse staff – should be shown as a fixed overhead; they are known as *indirect labour*.

As with the rent, your legal fees, your audit fee, your bank interest, your equipment depreciation, insurance premiums, light, heat, telephone and stationery should all be calculated on a monthly basis, regardless of when these items fall due for payment. Sometimes there is a considerable time lag. Take the audit fee, for example. By inference, it will be well into the following year of trading before you have to pay your first year's audit fee, but provision must be made in that first year for the cost of having your figures audited at the year end.

Dealing with your promotional costs is not easy. The most conservative accounting treatment is to write off expenditure as and when it is incurred, with no attempt to compare promotional costs with the revenue generated. Although prudent, this method of accounting will produce misleading losses in a build up period and the figures projected on this basis will not be terribly helpful. It is more realistic to charge advertising and mailing costs in the months in which sales will be generated. If you send out an autumn brochure at the end of August for instance, the whole of the costs of that mailing, from photography through to printing and postage, might be written off 40 per cent in September, 40 per cent in October and 20 per cent in November. An advertisement has a much shorter life and should be charged in the month it appears, or at most spread partly into the following month. You therefore should calculate, both in the case of a brochure and an advertisement, over what sort of period you expect to receive sales, and then you must split the total costs over that selling period. Inevitably, before you begin generating sales – that is, before the advertisement appears or the brochure is despatched – you will be incuring costs in the form of photography, artwork, etc. As far as your profit plan is concerned, these costs should be held in suspense until they can be matched with the sales they will generate.

6. Having carefully listed the overheads for each month, you should deduct them from the gross profit, and the figure left is your net profit – or, if the overheads are higher than your gross profit, your *net loss*.

The cash forecast

With the estimating done, the cash forecast is something which should flow naturally from the assumptions you have made in the profit plan. Basically, it is a question of taking each item of income and expenditure itemised in the profit plan and judging which month the income will actually come into the bank and in which month payments will have to be made. Below are a few guidelines.

Sales We think it probably reasonable to say that most mail order businesses tend to be cash businesses. This, of course, makes things very simple. Your monthly income figure will remain the same as on the profit plan.

Cost of sales This is simply a question of applying what credit terms you have secured from your suppliers. Do bear in mind, however, that you will need an initial stock for each new brochure and advertisement, which may have to be paid for before sales start to flow.

Labour obviously falls due for payment in the month in which it is employed, but do not forget the PAYE and National Insurance contributions. These have to be deducted from staff wages and salaries, but are not remitted to the Collector of Taxes until the following month. This effectively spreads about 30 per cent of the gross payroll into the following month.

Overheads Your overheads, of course, will look vastly different when apportioned in cash-flow terms. Suppose, for example, you are leasing a van. Three months' rental will be required in advance and then there is a full year's insurance premium to be paid. This will make the first month or two look very different indeed from the profit plan. Against this, of course, items like bank interest and legal and professional charges tend to accumulate and are paid in arrears.

As far as promotional costs are concerned, for cash-flow purposes these must now be recorded when they fall due for payment. If you are able to negotiate credit terms with your printer and/or advertising agency, it could be that you do not have to pay the bulk of your costs until you have started to generate sales. However, items such as model fees, photography and design work are likely to be paid well in advance of the sales to which they should be allocated. Bearing in mind that promotional spending is going to be such a heavy item within your overheads, it is important to plot it accurately, since it is clearly going to have a dramatic effect on your bank balance.

Capital expenditure For cash forecasting purposes, you need some additional headings for capital expenditure. In the first few months, these figures may be high. Again, as with every other item in the cash forecast, only reflect these capital items in the month in which they are actually paid for. If you have any regular loan repayments, these can be recorded under the heading of capital expenditure.

In your profit plan you will have excluded VAT from your sales figures and all of the costs. For cash forecasting purposes you will need to increase the receipts by the amount of VAT which is included. You will also need to increase the payments to allow for the costs which bear VAT. It is probable that your initial spending on equipment and stock will give rise to a VAT refund within the first three or four months. Thereafter you will almost certainly need to allow for a quarterly payment of VAT (the difference between the VAT included in your sales and the VAT charged by your suppliers).

Probably you will find that your cash forecast begins several weeks, if not months, before your profit plan. Initially the cash forecast will all go one way – more than likely in the accumulation of an overdraft! Gradually, however, once you start feeding in sales, and your first year's trading starts to develop, you will see your bank balance swoop up and down, reflecting the peaks and troughs.

The mechanics of cash-flow In a cash forecast you are not concerned with profit. It is purely the money in the bank in which you are interested. You head up your chart with receipts (that is, sales, VAT refunds – anything that represents income) and then use the rest of the page to list the various deductions (any payments out) as they fall due each month. You will end up with two figures – cash in and cash out. Update the starting cash balance (or overdraft) by the net figure of inflow or outflow for each month and you will produce a monthly forecast of your cash/overdraft position. This will indicate your working capital requirement.

This may seem like an awfully tedious exercise, but it really is vital. So many potentially good businesses fail in their early stages through being under-capitalised. This occurs simply because they had not appreciated that it would take time to move into profitability and produce positive cash-flow. In an expanding new business, particularly in mail order, a continuing build-up of stock and capital investment may well produce an adverse cash-flow for some months, despite the fact that profits are being produced. Sometimes it may take a couple of years or more before the cash-flow starts moving in the right direction.

Losses cost money and they are much easier to finance when they are anticipated and planned for. If you prepare a realistic profit plan and cash forecast, which shows that you are going to make consistent losses, or will need to finance the build-up of stock and the advance payment for advertising and brochure costs for the first six months, you may a find that a bank manager will be prepared to support you because you have quite clearly done your homework and know where you are going. If you sell the same bank manager a rosy picture of instant profit, you may get the much smaller overdraft you think you require, but what happens when you are four or five months into losses and way over your overdraft facility? At that point your frightened bank manager may well ask for a receiver to be appointed. Your bank manager would not have reacted like that if he had known what to expect. Take tremendous time and trouble with your profit plan. Go over and over it until you are absolutely sure that you have it as right as it can be. Believe us when we say it is the key to your success – or failure.

From these projections you will have established two things. First, whether you can make a profit and, second, how much money you will need to finance your venture. It has to be said that mail order businesses do not easily attract bank support. We think you should realise that the money you invest initially will either have to be your own, or that of a partner. Once you have established a track record, once you can take along a brochure or an advertisement to a bank manager and demonstrate how much money it has generated, then you should be able to arrange a loan to finance expansion. Initially, though, if you have no other business to back up your mail order venture, then you are going to have a long, hard slog in order to build bank confidence.

After sounding so depressing on the subject of finance, we would alert you to the various government schemes that are available for helping small businesses, and would suggest you contact your local Department of Trade, Small Firms Division, who will be able to give you full information as to what schemes are available in your area. The DHSS are helpful here, too.

If you are unable to raise any additional finance, you will simply have to use what capital you have available, invest it carefully, hopefully to make a profit, and plough that profit straight back into further advertising. Once you can demonstrate that your goods actually do sell by mail order, then take all the facts and figures along to your bank manager, together with a profit plan and cash forecast, and you should be given some support.

16. Systems, control and administration

In mail order traders' heaven, a transaction with a customer would go something like this. She would send in her order, neatly written out, with her address in full, including postcode. Included with the order would be her cheque, or credit card number. The cheque would be signed. In the case of a credit card, the number would be correct. The order would be processed, the goods would be in stock and despatched within the stipulated period. The goods would be received, undamaged, and would be precisely what the customer required. The interesting thing about the situation we have just described is that this is most people's idea of what is involved in running a mail order business. One of the main reasons we have written this book is because we are aware that most people assume it is an easy business to run – when in reality it is very far from that.

Every small business needs controls and a good administrative system, so that it can operate efficiently. In mail order, these controls have to be on a far more grandiose scale than perhaps is immediately apparent. Let us return to our mythical customer. Any of the following permutations can, and all too often, do happen. When she sent in her order form she could have left it incomplete, so that a telephone call is necessary to establish which colour or size she requires. She could have sent a cheque and not signed it, ticked the box for a Barclaycard debit, but forgotten to fill in her number. Several days after the receipt of the order, when it is already packed and dispatched, she may well change her mind and telephone to say she would like her order amended. On receipt of the goods, she may want them replaced; desire a refund; want a mixture of the two; and/or in the light of the goods she has received, if there are still some items outstanding, yet to be delivered, she may want to amend the order in some way. When she receives her replacement goods, she may still not like them. When she receives her refund cheque, she may claim it is not enough because she has lost the original catalogue stating the price . . . etc. etc.

You may think we are exaggerating. Believe us – we are not. I (Deborah) remember very early on in our business receiving a large order from a woman who had several small children. It was one of those orders on which there was a jinx. We kept sending garments which kept coming back. She either wanted a bigger size, or a smaller size, or a different colour. Finally, after endless transactions backwards and forwards, we came to the point where satisfactory goods appeared to have been delivered. Then we had yet another letter, this time telling us that one of the pairs of dungarees she had been sent she had decided to sell to her neighbour, since they were not quite right for her own little boy. The neighbour, apparently, would be sending us a cheque direct (the neighbour's name was not mentioned, of course) and therefore our beloved customer still had £9.95 or whatever in credit and so therefore would like a sweater. The sweater turned out to be not quite as she had imagined and so it came back, too. I remember sending her a refund cheque by return just in case she tried to order anything else. I was absolutely hysterical by that time!

Of course, a great many customers' orders are entirely straightforward and, if your service and product are good, then your transactions, naturally, are likely to be more trouble free. Nevertheless, it should be realised how important it is to keep accurate records on all forms of communication with your customers – and it is not easy!

We thought the best way to deal with the many and varying elements that go together to create a mail order administrative system would be to break them down under as many headings as possible, which we have done, as follows.

GENERAL BOOK-KEEPING AND CONTROL

Whatever type of business you are running, you have to find a formula for keeping control! Book-keeping is a chore in most small businesses, but it has to be done. We would go so far as to say that you cannot have a responsible attitude towards your business unless you keep adequate records. In the previous chapter, we tried to demonstrate that you do not need to be a chartered accountant in order to produce a cash forecast and profit plan. Likewise you do not need to be particularly numerate to understand and introduce basic, simple book-keeping and control systems. Book-keeping falls into two categories: the requirements of the outside world and those internal controls which you need for your own benefit in order to manage your business. In dealing with the outside world, you require records for your bank, your customers, your suppliers, the VAT man, the tax man – both PAYE and business tax and the DHSS – both for national insurance and statutory sick pay. The records you require for internal use will cover stock control, costing, performance and list maintenance.

In a book about mail order it would be quite wrong to go into the details of double entry book-keeping in any depth. However, what follows are a few thoughts on the basic principles of control – control of any business – which we hope will prove useful.

Let us look first at accounting for your dealings with the outside world, under the headings already mentioned.

The bank

To keep control of your bank balance, it is essential that you have a cash book which records on one side the receipts and, on the other, the payments you make. The cash book should be kept up to date *every day*. In other words, you must enter the cheques drawn and details of your takings. An important point on mail order credits: normally, when you pay a cheque into the bank, you are expected to list the payee's name against the amount. If you are paying vast numbers of cheques into the bank, this is simply not possible – no one has the time. Arrange with your bank that you can submit customer cheques, supported by an adding machine print out, itemising the cheques by amount only.

At least every month you must check your cash book entries against your bank statement and reconcile the bank statement against your cash book balance. Ask for weekly bank statements, they help you to keep control far better than monthly ones. Routine is what you need. You, or someone in your office, should produce a bank balance every Monday morning and you should never go home at night until the cash book is written up.

Customers

Whilst we appreciate that there are some mail order companies who offer credit terms, they all are almost exclusively the big boys. As far as you are concerned, we recommend that you should not even consider doing so. There is no way you can start a mail order business from scratch on any basis other than *cash with order*. This being the case, your relationship with customers is dealt with under the 'Order processing' section later in this chapter.

Suppliers

If your suppliers are few and you only receive a small number of invoices each month, you can keep track of them by having a file of *unpaid* invoices in your top drawer and *paid* invoices in your bottom drawer. As and when you pay for goods, you simply move the unpaid copy from your top to bottom drawer. If your transactions are numerous, you need a purchase journal to list and analyse the invoices and a purchase ledger to record invoices and settlement on each supplier's account. The purchase ledger should be kept up to date at least weekly and agreed with the suppliers' statements at least monthly. As far as possible, pay against statements rather than invoices.

VAT

Unless your sales are below the VAT threshold, or your goods zerorated, you need to charge VAT to your customers and pay it quarterly to HM Customs and Excise. Your cash book should be analysed to identify the VAT content of your sales. Likewise, the VAT charged to you on virtually all your purchases and expenses should be identified in your cash book – and, if appropriate, your purchase journal – so it can be deducted from your quarterly statement. VAT returns are always looked on as things of dread. If, however, you keep up-to-date records, your VAT return should take no longer than quarter of an hour to produce. There's a challenge.

Tax

PAYE is more of a nuisance than a difficulty, but it is unavoidable. If you are paying just yourself and your spouse, simply use the Inland Revenue standard forms for your records. If you employ half a dozen people, invest in a small multi-copy payroll system – Safeguard is the best, in our view. If you are employing over twenty people, then subcontract the hassle to a local computer bureau. They are not expensive for this type of service.

Tax on the business will be based on your annual accounts, but make sure your books and your filing are up to date so that the information your accountants need is available without a major research programme being mounted. This, apart from anything else, is expensive.

The DHSS

National Insurance administration is part and parcel of the weekly, or monthly, payroll routine and tends to be dealt with in conjunction with PAYE. The need for adequate personal records and files has been underlined by the recent introduction of the Statutory Sick Pay Scheme and you must now keep records for all your employees.

So this is what you *have* to do. Now let us look at what you *should* do. There is far more to keeping control than having a minimum level of up-to-date financial books and records. They will, to a large extent, tell you where you are. What they will not tell you is where you should have been, nor where you have been, nor where you are going! You need internal controls for your own benefit. Let us examine these one by one.

Stock

We will be dealing with stock and the particular problems it causes in mail order later in this chapter. However, it is important to stress that many a company has failed through carrying too much or the wrong stock and never can an industry be more in danger of this happening than the mail order industry. Accurate records are vital, not only so that you can ensure your customer can be serviced properly, but also so that you know precisely where you are when it comes to ordering and re-ordering materials or finished goods.

Costing

This is an area which is vital to the running of any business. But in the case of mail order it is particularly important, since the size of your promotional spend is so large that it must be counterbalanced by realistic profits. Of course, the price you charge your customer may not necessarily be based on your costs. In certain circumstances, you may be able to obtain a very high gross profit, your pricing policy being based on what the market will stand. In the first section of the book we dealt with costing in some detail. Suffice to say here that you must keep rigid control of your direct costs, constantly reassessing them to make sure that they are on plan.

Performance

Having acquired an adequate and sensible set of records, what should you be doing with them? How can you use them to tell you what you need to know? Basically, you should be able to use them to provide you with a performance record, to measure what you have achieved, what is currently happening and what you should be doing in the future. Adequate records of this sort will enable you to avoid disasters and help you react positively when an opportunity presents itself. We believe that every business should produce a profit plan, at least annually, and prepare monthly management accounts within two or three weeks of the end of each month. Monthly management accounts consist of at least a trading statement and a balance sheet. The trading statement should follow the same basic format as your profit plan, but instead of forecasting you plot the *actual* figures each month. These, of course, should be compared with the profit plan to see if you are meeting your targets. The balance sheet is purely a statement of the assets and liabilities of your business at that particular time and it is important that the figures should be measured against what you expected the position to be.

As your business grows, inevitably you will start employing staff. The bigger the business, the more you are in danger of losing control. You have to know what is going on.

> How many orders did you receive last week?
> How many inquiries for brochures?
> How much do you owe Bloggs and Co.?
> What is the size of your overdraft?
> What is the return rate on that particular product?
> How much did you pay for your last batch of raw materials?
> Why are the postage costs so high this month?

You must keep in touch with this type of detail and the only way you can do it is to maintain adequate records. An efficiently run, well-controlled company benefits externally as well as internally. For example, as your business builds, if your orders are delivered on time and if your quality is consistent, your customer list will grow. Then even if they see items of a similar nature for sale at a cheaper price than yours, they are unlikely to take the risk of changing allegiance.

Similarly, if your staff see that you are efficient, then they tend to become efficient too. Stringent stock control not only ensures good customer service, it will also reduce staff pilferage. It has to be true: a ship is only as good as her captain.

So keep control at all times. The more successful you are, the more vulnerable you are. The more you prosper, the more you become reliant on other people, and the more remote you are from the action. So be prepared. However small your business is now, set up the controls that will stand the test of time. They can literally be worth their weight in gold.

ORDER PROCESSING

In this section we are covering the administrative *requirements* of running a mail order business. How we cope with these requirements, we will deal later on in this chapter. We have sub-divided the process as below.

Receipt of order

On arrival of a customer's order, whether by post or telephone, the first consideration is whether it can be met now, or at any time in the future. If the goods are in stock, then the order can be processed – that is, the cheque paid in, or the credit card charged, and the order sent through to Despatch. If the goods are not in stock, then either the customer must be informed and her cheque returned, or, if the goods are expected, the order can be put *on hold* and acknowledged, giving the customer a delivery date.

139

Processing of order

Once the order is released for processing, there are various people who will need to know what has happened to it. First of all, the Despatch Department will clearly need details of the order and despatch documentation. This documentation should take the form of an address label to stick on the customer's parcel, instructions for the despatcher as to what promotional materials should be included in the customer's parcel, and a piece of paper for the despatcher to sign, indicating the date on which the goods are sent.

Second, the person or department responsible for customer relations will need to know the moment the goods have been despatched, so that they can answer any query should the customer ring or write regarding the order. Third, the warehouse staff should be informed that the order has been despatched, so that the stock can be adjusted accordingly.

Return of order

When goods are returned, it will be for one of two reasons. Either that the customer simply does not like what you have sent, or there is something wrong with the goods. If the latter is the case, then you need a system set up so that something can be done about the faulty goods in question. If they have been supplied to you by a manufacturer, then you need return documentation so that you, too, can reclaim your money. If you are manufacturing the item yourself, then it should be sent back to Quality Control for investigation. Either way, it is very important that a record is kept of *why* goods have been returned. Returns are very bad for a mail order business: they lose custom and they cost a great deal of money. Inevitably, returns fall into a pattern, which will become recognisable if proper records are maintained. Once you have established a pattern you will know what steps to take to reduce your rate of return.

Remember, too, that you must have some form of documentation for putting non-faulty goods back into stock.

Replacement of order

Goods to be replaced should follow exactly the same procedure as a first-time order, except that in some way they should be identified as replacements, so that they receive priority treatment. If customers have had to return goods, for whatever reason, they are far more impatient about receiving a replacement than they would be about a first-time order. In fairness to them, you also need to recognise that you will have been holding on to their money for some time, without their benefiting from the goods. So, on moral grounds, the replacement order should be given priority. Again, once it is despatched, it is important that all departments are informed.

Refund of order

Refunds must be dealt with quickly and efficiently. Just because the goods are not satisfactory and the customer has asked for a refund, it does not mean that he or she will never order from you again. In fact quite the contrary. If the refund is efficiently and promptly dealt with, it will actually build customer confidence so that they will not hesitate to order again, since they now have the security of knowing they will receive their refund if the goods are again unsatisfactory.

We found it best in the case of refunds to operate a completely separate bank account, into which money was transferred from time to time. We also realised that neither ourselves nor our accountant had the time to sign refund cheques and we therefore appointed a trusted member of staff to do this for us. She had a maximum signatory value of £100, and anything over that had to be countersigned by a director. The alternative to this is to have pre-printed cheques, already signed, though obviously these have to be kept very carefully under lock and key. Refund documentation is important. You need a payment slip to accompany the cheque with a note inviting the customer to order again. You need the information to be passed through to Customer Relations, so that any queries can be dealt with, and you need the cheques carefully recorded as to VAT content.

So, you can see that a great deal of organisation is required to keep information and goods flowing, to ensure that the customer is properly serviced and that you have the back-up records to study trends and reactions.

INTERPRETING RESPONSE

The process by which orders are received and goods despatched is of course the backbone of the business, but interpreting the details of this process is also very important. The major requirement is to be able to forecast stock requirements and unfortunately this is something which can only be tackled with experience. Once you have started to build up an order pattern – whether by native cunning or with the aid of a computer – you will have a yardstick by which you can compare future promotions. Detailed forecasting is vitally important and you need to gather together as much statistical information as you can on response to your various advertisements and mailings so that you can begin to gauge reaction with some kind of accuracy.

If you are going to employ the use of a computer for this exercise, do be careful not to rely on it too heavily. Remember, it is only a machine without any powers of original thought. By way of example, I (Deborah) worked for a while for a mail order company which had an enormous success with leg warmers in one of its catalogues. The computer estimated on the experience of previous successes that for the next catalogue a very minimum of 3,000 pairs should be bought as an initial stock, with an option on a further 6,000. This instruction was duly carried out, the leg warmers bought and delivered. Only then did someone realise the absurdity of what had happened: *this massive purchase of leg warmers had been bought for a summer catalogue*! It sounds farcical, but it is surprisingly easy for such a thing to happen.

Interpreting response is enormously important when it comes to ensuring that enough of the right stock is available to meet demand. It is also a vital tool to use in gauging trends. We touched briefly on this in the previous section, when we stressed the importance of finding out the reasons *why* goods are returned. This is certainly one area where interpreting response is important, but there is so much more information you need to gather: which is your most popular size, your most popular colour and, very important, which of your goods represents the best use of space? To explain what we mean by that, we will cite an example. We did an exercise in one of our catalogues where we directly related the amount of space allocated to each item against the number of sales made. To our astonishment, we found that a dress at the bottom of page six, allocated space of approximately two inches square, had made the most money pro rata with the space allocated. In the next catalogue, we changed the colour of the dress and put it up with the known best-sellers. *It took more money than any of them*. It was a best-seller all the time, hidden away, without our even realising it.

Success in mail order depends so much on testing series of different formulas and then using the best. This is the value of interpreting response. So keep a flexibility of mind and look out for the many different ways of finding out as much as you can about your customers' reaction to your products.

STOCK AND SUPPLIERS

This is a hoary subject and the area which causes more trouble than any other in mail order. The fact is that, if you have a wildly successful promotion, the chances are that it will throw you into dreadful dramas over your ability to fulfil orders. If you have sufficient stock to meet your demands, chances are that you are equally in trouble because your promotions are not pulling enough. You dare not stock as much as you would like to, in case the promotion does not work, and yet you dare not stock too little, in case it does!

The key to success, of course, is good suppliers. You need to convince them that as well as putting in to you an initial stock, they should also hold a made-up stock in reserve and have options on whatever raw materials they need for further supplies if your promotion goes mad. It may be helpful to get involved with your suppliers' suppliers, and possibly take up an option yourself on raw material. If you are a manufacturer, things are easier – up to a point. Certainly the stock you hold can be in an unfinished, or semi-finished state, to be completed as orders come in. However, do bear in mind that a highly successful promotion will strain your business *on all levels*. With administrative resources generally stretched, you do not want to find yourself unable to cope with manufacture.

An extreme example of this was our very first Sunday supplement advertisement. It was an enormous success, but on Day 1 of receiving orders we were not able to start manufacture, because it required literally all our staff just to open the post! This was a situation we made sure was never repeated, but it goes to demonstrate what an enormous impact a highly successful promotion can have.

The various codes of practice demand that you have a reasonable stock before you advertise a product, but *reasonable* is not really the problem here – it is a matter of having the *right* stock. For this reason, do not have too many choices of item, at least until you have considerable experience. In other words, do not offer an item in three colours if you can offer it in one. The fashion trade is the most notorious for stock-building – think of all those different sizes as well as colours! Our thirty-two-page brochure, which we put out twice a year, had 3,000 different permutations. It is horrifying how much money you have to tie up to service that sort of range.

Try to be clever about your stock. Supposing you have a line which sells quite well, but you feel is played out, and yet you still have a little stock. Try rephotographing it and giving it a tiny space in your next catalogue. Hopefully, if you gauge it right, you will receive just enough orders to clear the stock. Do not be afraid to recognise a loser. There is no point in having dusty shelves full of stock which will never sell and, far worse, it is the kiss of death to fill your catalogue full of anything other than products which you believe to be winners. If an item is not selling, get rid of the stock. Sell it at a loss – on a market stall, to a fellow trader, anything, but clear it out and start again, having carefully been through a soul-searching exercise to decide why it happened. No one puts together a catalogue of anything other than what they believe to be winners, but the fact is that some items will work and some will not. You must be prepared to recognise when you have backed a loser – in which case the best thing to do is to get out fast.

Sale leaflets can work quite well sometimes to clear stock. You should try mailing your regular customers with a limited offer, explaining first come, first served, and that cheques will be returned if the goods are sold out. Be careful of this exercise, however, from a costing point of view. Do your costings carefully and make sure that it would not be better to simply sell off the items through the trade, rather than launch an expensive mail order operation. The stock you have left is bound to be made up largely of the least popular item, colour, size, or whatever – you will be dealing in residue. It is not really the best basis on which to launch a mail order campaign.

A final note on suppliers. Unless you are in the position to buy ahead in very large quantities, you must pick reputable suppliers. Tie them down in writing and make sure they understand the implications of a mail order business and how vital it is to have goods delivered on time.

CUSTOMER LISTS

A good mailing list is the cornerstone of your business. Without it, you will never make money in mail order. Many a business has failed simply because its principals have failed to realise the importance of their list and have either been slovenly in its maintenance or appear to attach no importance to it at all.

We have talked at some length about the pros and cons of buying other people's lists. Here we are looking purely at the maintenance of your own. Every mailing list should be sub-divided into two main sections: your buyers and your prospects. Let us look at these in some detail.

The buyers' list

In the early days of your business everyone who has ever bought from you will go on this list. Gradually, as time goes by, you will need to recognise that some names clearly represent a one-off purchase only and should either be dropped altogether or put on your prospects list. Different mail order companies take different views. Some keep non-responsive buyers on a list for two years, some for six months. Rather than consider the time factor, the most relevant aspect should be how many times you have mailed a name without response. Certainly, after four or five mailings, if no response has been forthcoming, you are probably wasting your money.

Your buyers' list will be constantly updated. As each day's orders come in, the information – not just the name and address, but also details of the order – should be put on file, so that you have a complete record on each of your customers. The information you need is name, address, postcode, telephone number, order value, what product was purchased, date of purchase and how the order was paid for (whether by cash or credit card). Initially you may not feel that all this information is necessary, but, as your mailing techniques become more sophisticated, you may well want to mail a certain sector of your list who have ordered a particular product. As we have mentioned in previous chapters, it is important that your mailing list is recorded in postal rebate order, so that at any time it can be called up and mailed in the most economic way possible.

You will see we are talking as though you are putting your mailing list on computer. Frankly there is no alternative. When we first started out in mail order, computer technology was in its infancy and would have been quite incapable of handling a mailing list of any size without massive capital investment in equipment. We had a system which, strangely enough, was quite effective in a homespun way. We had cards printed and across the top we had a series of perforated squares with holes in them. The cards were kept in a card index box, quoting customer's name and address, and order details, just as we have outlined. When we wanted to pull out all the buyers, we selected the square along the top of the card which represented buyers and pushed a knitting needle through the hole. Those cards which represented buyers had their perforated square removed so that as we lifted the cards clear from the card index tray, the buyers fell out in a heap!

Mail order, Fowler style, circa early 1970s, is certainly not relevant today, but the principle remains the same. Your list needs to be filed in such a way that you can get access to any part or portion of it at any time, particularly those of your customers who buy from you regularly.

The prospects list

This list will have evolved from a number of different sources. Some of the names will be people who have sent for your catalogue and subsequently never ordered. They may be the residue from a bought-in list, who never purchased anything from you. They may be names from a newspaper competition, who you have yet to mail, names rejected from your buyers' list, people you have lifted from specific telephone directories – or compiled from a variety of sources. This list should be mailed from time to time; once a customer has bought, then he or she is automatically transferred to the buyers' file.

This is the list we would recommend you use for mailing swaps and renting. Whilst it may not turn in anything like the response of your buyers' file, if you keep it regularly maintained it should produce a reasonable response rate.

.This brings us to the question of list maintenance which is all important. Supposing you did not open your address book for a year. When eventually you did, you would find that several of your friends had moved house, married or remarried, left the country or come back. A mailing list is no different; it is just on a bigger scale. The automatic insertion of all orders into your buyers' list will ensure that these people are kept up to date in terms of details. However, what about the others? Every time you send out a mailing a number of envelopes will be returned to you with 'gone away', or 'name and address unknown' on them. From time to time, customers will write to you and advise you of their change of address or tell you that for some reason they no longer require your catalogue. To take an example of this, as suppliers of children's clothes, from time to time we used to receive very sad letters, advising us that a child had died and that parents were therefore very anxious to receive no more mailings. In these circumstances, it was obviously extremely important that the name was eradicated from the list.

All such changes should be accumulated over a period of time and, before a fresh mailing, the mailing list should be 'cleaned' of all these names. With regard to this exercise, do bear in mind the point we made when discussing the merging and purging process. Even if it is one name that you need taken out of your file, the fact is that you have to run your entire mailing list for that particular area against it in order to ensure that it has been removed. It is a costly business, so do try to combine a series of activities when cleaning the list. For example, you might be planning to compare someone else's list with your own, in which case it would be possible to include your own cleaning operation at the same time. Look at ways of cost saving. Whilst a list needs looking after, it should be done so as economically as possible.

One of the other main problems of a mailing list is duplication. Because of the precise way in which a computer works, it can easily record the same person twice, three, four, even five times, simply because the name or address is very slightly different – for example, two initials instead of one, with a postcode or without. Such duplication is going to cost you an unnecessarily large sum of money, sending several mailing packages to the same person. Moreover, there is the irritation factor. Who wants to receive several copies of the same catalogue? Also it will place in the customer's mind a feeling of doubt as to your efficiency. If several mailing packages are received by one person, the chances are they probably will not order from you for fear of being the recipient of another administrative snarl-up.

One final word on mailing lists. As a mail order company, you must recognise that your single biggest asset is your mailing list. You could be forgiven for thinking otherwise, since this is a view that is not generally shared outside the mail order industry. Try persuading the average bank manager that your mailing list is worth quarter of a million pounds, or whatever. He may be aware that it produces you a million pounds' worth of turnover a year, but his attitude will be that this does not represent an asset of any long-term note. In North America and most of Europe, the commercial community is more enlightened as to the value of mailing lists, and it is only a matter of time before the business establishment of this country begin to appreciate their true worth. So guard your mailing list carefully. It represents the future of your business.

COMPUTERS

Let us return to mail order traders' heaven. As well as having the ideal customer, one would also like to have the ideal system to deal with orders. The ideal system? One, which at the touch of a button will tell you, on receipt of an order, whether you have the goods in stock; where the punching in of an order will not only produce despatch documentation but update the mailing list, adjust the stock position and produce a print-out sheet for the customer relations department. Similarly, if the order is returned, punching it into the machine will ensure that the stock is credited, a refund cheque printed, the mailing list informed and the customer relations department advised of the transaction.

Such systems do exist. In fact the top dozen or so mail order companies in this country have such a system. For the rest of us, it is a question of compromise.

One of the biggest mistakes that you can make in the setting up of a mail order business is to assume that you can buy a computer to handle all your administrative requirements. All right, if you have unlimited cash then this is possible, as we have just described. However, the kind of machine you need is not a sort of glorified home computer, costing somewhere between £2,000 and £10,000. It simply will not do the job, – in fact it is worse than useless. You must recognise that in the early days of your mail order business you should be looking to the services of a computer bureau.

Initially your very first requirement will be to set up a mailing list. Thereafter you need to look at order processing, which can perfectly well be handled by a bureau rather than dealt with in-house. Only when you are really certain of the direction in which your business is moving, and have analysed precisely what information you require from a computer, should you even contemplate putting in your own system.

Let us look what a computer bureau will do for you, apart from looking after your list. First, on a daily basis, you can pass your orders to a bureau (here you have a logistics problem – it is important to find one not too far from you). From these orders the bureau will produce the following for you.

1. Despatch documentation in the form of a master sheet and self-adhesive labels. Most bureaux will be able to produce this documentation in such a way that it is easy to despatch. In other words, all the like products will be batched together, even down to size and colour where appropriate.

2. Daily, weekly, or perhaps twice weekly, the bureau will produce an alphabetical list of customers, against which will be their order and up-to-date despatch information. It should be noted that the Despatch Department will return completed despatch documentation to the bureau so that they can include despatch details on these alphabetical print-outs. This is the document which is used by the Customer Relations Department to check on customers' orders.

3. The new orders will be added to the mailing list.

4. From the order processing, a range of statistical information will be available, which it will be up to you to select. This involves the summarising of orders by product, by source, or however you want it presented. This information will serve to help you with forecasting.

If you so wish, a computer bureau can also help you with returns – producing documentation for a replacement, or, in the case of a refund, a cheque and payment advice slip. This is one of the excellent aspects of using a computer bureau: you can take advantage of as much, or as little, of the service they have to offer, as is compatible with your own facilities. As far as finding computer bureaux is concerned, we would suggest you subscribe to *Direct Response Magazine*, which is published by Macro Publishing Ltd. Their address is given at the end of the book. You will find a list of computer bureaux in *Direct Response Magazine*, as well as a great deal of other helpful information. However, before committing yourself to a particular bureau, we would suggest that you take up references.

It is very difficult to generalise when it comes to advising you about the administration of your mail order business. If you already have an existing business – perhaps you are a manufacturer or a retailer, selling by traditional means – then you already have established systems and staff. If you have an existing warehouse and warehouse staff, clearly it would be relatively easy for you to enlarge this to include mail order despatch. Similarly, you may have an existing computer system which, whilst it may not have a large enough memory to hold your mailing list, could perhaps perform some role – whether it is producing despatch documentation or refund cheques.

In an attempt to come down off the fence and offer specific advice, we would say this: if you are setting up a mail order company from scratch, without the benefit of an existing business, then we would suggest that you sub-contract every possible element of your mail order operation – from order processing to actual despatch of goods. The reason for this is twofold. First, the services of computer bureaux and fulfilment houses will instantly provide you with expertise, where you yourself may well have none. As well as providing the actual function for which you will be paying them, you will also find that you will learn a great deal from them. This means that when, and if, you do come to set up your own system, you have at least learnt how it should be operated. Second, it is all too easy within a mail order business for overheads to run away with you. You might begin with yourself, your spouse, partner or friend, and then start adding staff as orders begin to flow. Before you know where you are, you could end up with substantial industrial premises and a staff of twenty. This will put you in the unsatisfactory position of having to undertake regular promotions, simply to pay your overheads. If you are sub-contracting the bulk of your operation, then each element of cost can be expressed individually on a per unit basis. In other words, you will be able to work out that it costs you, say, 75p to process an order and 55p to have it despatched. These then, are not fixed costs, as they only apply when you make a sale. It is a far safer way of operating, particularly in the early stages.

Of course, right at the very beginning of your operation you may well have to operate on a cottage industry basis, because you are not processing enough orders to make it worth while for a computer to become involved. However, the moment you can make the transfer, do so. There are enough risk factors involved in the mail order business without adding to them. So to succeed, initially, you want the very minimum of commitment so far as overheads are concerned.

Conclusion

So what have we left to say in conclusion? Possibly, just this: *never, never underestimate mail order – on any level*. When it works, it can make you very rich indeed; when it goes wrong, your business can move into a downward spiral with lightning speed – and the margin between these two extremes is surprisingly slender.

In some types of business, after trading a while you can reach a safe plateau, where you can relax a little, confident of turning in a regular if unexciting profit, year in, year out. Not so in mail order. Just because your last brochure was a success, it does not mean the next will be. Each new promotion tests afresh you, your products, your marketing expertise. Yes, mail order is stimulating, terrifying, exhilarating, infuriating, volatile and, despite all the planning in the world, frighteningly unpredictable. Above all, it is not a business for the faint-hearted.

Good luck!

Useful addresses

Advertising Standards
Authority
Code of Advertising Practice
Committee
2–16 Torrington Place
London WC1E 7HN
01–580 5555

Association of Mail Order
Publishers
1 Burlington Street
London W1X 1FP
01–437 0706

British Direct Marketing
Association
1 New Oxford Street
London W1A 1NQ
01–242 2254

Creative Handbook
100 St Martin's Lane
London WC2N 4AZ
01–379 7399

Distribution Services
Ltd
Head Office
Elstree Way
Boreham Wood
Herts WD6 1JQ
01–953 1661

Hollis Press and Public
Relations Annual
Contact House
Sunbury-on-Thames T16 5HG
(09327) 84781

Independent Broadcasting
Authority
70 Brompton Road
London SW3 1EY
01–584 7011

Independent Television
Companies Association
56 Mortimer Street
London W1N 8AN
01–636 6866

Institute of Practitioners in
Advertising
44 Belgrave Square
London SW1X 8QS
01–235 7020

Institute of Public Relations
Gatehouse
St John's Square
London EC1M 4DH
01–253 5151

Lex Wilkinson Ltd
Head Office
King's House
King's Street
Bedworth
Near Coventry CV12 8LL
(0203) 310515

Macro Publishing Ltd
41b High Street
Hoddesdon
Herts EN11 8TA
(0992) 469556

Newspaper Publishers'
Association
16 Took's Court
London EC4A 1LB
01–405 6806

Newspaper Society
6 Carmelite Street
London WC4 0BY
01–583 3311

Periodical Publishers'
Association
Imperial House
15–19 Kingsway
London WC2B 6UN
01–379 6268

Scottish Daily Newspaper
Society
50 George Square
Glasgow G2 1RR
041–552 4994

Scottish Newspaper Proprietors'
Association
3–11 North St Andrew's Street
Edinburgh EH2 1JU
031–557 3600

Securicor Ltd
Head Office
15 Gillingham Street
London SW1V 1HZ
01–828 5611

Tibbett and Britten Ltd
Head Office
691–7 High Road
London NI7 8AZ
01–808 3040